Soul Purpose INC.

The Practical Guide to Living Your Faith at Work

CRAIG MCANDREWS

LUCIDBOOKS

Soul Purpose Inc.
The Practical Guide to Living Your Faith at Work

Copyright © 2018 by Craig McAndrews

Published by Lucid Books in Houston, TX
www.LucidBooksPublishing.com

ISBN-10: 1-63296-306-X
ISBN-13: 978-1-63296-306-2
eISBN-10: 1-63296-279-9
eISBN-13: 978-1-63296-279-9

Special Sales: Most Lucid Books titles are available in special quantity discounts. Custom imprinting or excerpting can also be done to fit special needs. Contact Lucid Books at Info@LucidBooksPublishing.com.

*Dedicated to the one who modeled working with
purpose and excellence, the risen Savior Jesus Christ.*

*"Work willingly at whatever you do, as though you were
working for the Lord rather than for people. Remember that
the Lord will give you an inheritance as your reward, and
that the Master you are serving is Christ" (Col. 3:23–24 NLT).*

Table of Contents

Introduction

Most of us spend more time at work than any other place in our lives. As a result, the workplace provides tremendous opportunity to interact with people and demonstrate our character in the way we live. What a great venue for living out the Christian faith! Unfortunately, many Christians downplay their faith at work and miss the abundant life Jesus has for them. The workplace is an under-developed mission field with enormous potential, a mission field ripe for the message of Jesus and the principles of the Bible. The workplace needs more Christians willing to step out of their comfort zone and into the opportunities to boldly live out their faith.

For some, the workplace may not be at an office—the work-from-home population is larger than ever—but either way, you're likely engaged with people, tackling projects, responding to emails, and performing a number of other tasks associated with your job. Work occupies a lot of our attention and our time. Unfortunately, many workplaces have either directly or indirectly made the topic of faith something to be avoided. Following a bit of the "separation of church and state" approach, workplaces often discourage faith-based activities or conversations. However, believers can respect the boundaries of any work environment while still reflecting their faith and making it a part of who they are at the office.

The workplace needs more integrity, compassion, willingness to serve, and even more love—and each of these principles is at the heart of the Christian faith. It seems as though every time we read the news, there is a new story of a business that has compromised some moral standard in the interest of improved profits or increased shareholder value. In many cases, these compromises might be committed by one person; however, the entire company shows up on the front page of the story. Where greed, selfishness, and pride often leave people asking themselves what's missing, the Christian faith offers the most compelling answer: Jesus Christ. Today's workplaces need more of what Jesus has to offer.

We need to bring our faith to work. Leaving it behind is like leaving your shoes at home when you go for a run. You might be able to finish the run, but it probably won't be your best time. Living a life in light of what the Bible teaches can be challenging—especially in today's world. Mainstream media and advertisements promote ideas contrary to what the Bible teaches. The world says that accumulation equals success; the Bible says that giving brings success. The world says to look out for yourself; the Bible says to look out for others. The world says to be happy; the Bible says to be holy. Over and over again we are bombarded by messages contradictory to what God planned for us. If our faith is absent from our work, then our lives will look no different from those who don't follow Jesus. If our faith is important to us, then it must be part of everything we do.

Prior to accepting Jesus as my Savior and surrendering my life to his leadership, I had a compartmental mentality. There was the home-self and the work-self. The home-self was more laid back, patient, and willing to help out where needed. The work-self was less patient and more driven for results. I was willing to help as long as there was something in it for me. My motivation to do anything at work was always connected to what I would get in return. I felt as though I needed to be a certain type of person to succeed at work, so I organized my life into neat compartments. I have come across many people who do this with their faith. Faith is OK on Sundays and select times during the week, but it rarely, if ever, shows up at work. They have bought into the same lie I bought into, a lie grounded in the perception of what it takes to be successful. Living this way doesn't work. In order to be all that God intends us to be, we must bring all of ourselves to what we do. The workplace is no different. Learning how to live our faith more openly at work will bring new meaning to what we do, and we will find renewed purpose in the place where we invest so much of our energy.

In Hebrews, the writer points out that the mature train their senses to determine what is good and what is bad (Heb. 5:14). What people of faith practice on a day in, day out basis matters. How we live our lives at work is a place of practice. The workplace can serve as a powerful arena for developing spiritual maturity as we live out our faith.

This book is about living your faith more boldly at work so that you might be part of what God wants to do in your life and in the lives around you. God is ready to work in and through you in a big way. His promises and his commands can be experienced at work in a way that impacts the eternity of people. When you consider working with purpose and meaning, what more could you ask for?

1

Work and Purpose

God has refined my faith more in my work than any other life arena. I've had my fair share of faith-filled moments and God-influenced refinement in every part of my life, but the workplace is where God has shaped my faith most profoundly.

I surrendered to Jesus early in my marriage, shortly after my first son was born, while starting a new business. There was a lot happening at the time. The business was where God's presence and influence was most magnified for me. Our new company started off great, and we had two solid years of positive growth and success. Unfortunately, we encountered major obstacles getting into the third year that wrecked much of what I had put my trust in. For starters, I always believed hard work was rewarded with success. Well, I had never worked harder or longer until that time, putting in the hours and making the sacrifices only to find our business on the verge of bankruptcy. Working harder wasn't helping.

I believed if I stayed organized and proactive, I could control the situation. That didn't happen. I was organized and paid great attention to the details, but over and over again things would happen that I couldn't anticipate. I was clearly not in control.

During that season of work, I realized the power of surrender. There was no question in my mind I could not manage myself through those sleep-deprived months of wondering when the next shoe would drop and the business would close. Even when I prayed and asked God to fix things, nothing changed. To borrow one of those traditional Christian sayings, I had to "let go and let God." It was a season of turning over control of every area of my life to the one who is in control anyway.

Eventually we sold our business, avoiding personal bankruptcy and the unpleasant circumstances that come with it. The downside was that I was 35 years old, unemployed, a new dad, and wondering what in the world I was going to do for a job. Then one day, the phone rang, and it was a friend of mine named Steve. He was running a business in Seattle, and asked if my business partner and I would come help him with a project. That project turned into another project, which turned into another, and opened the door to starting a consulting business.

The consulting stage was a huge shift from the retail business. We didn't have employees or any real estate to support. This business was a new way to make a living. During this season, I realized the power of God's provision. I had read my Bible, and knew that Philippians 4:19 said, "*And my God will supply all your needs according to His riches and glory in Christ Jesus,*" but I never knew what that really meant. In this case, it literally turned out to be *all* my needs. In the six years we operated that business, I never once made a formal sales call. I had plenty of conversations with follow-up requests or putting together a proposal, but I never had to find new business. It seemed as though every time projects were winding down (meaning finances were winding down), the phone would ring with a new opportunity. Over and over again, we were provided for. Unlike the previous stage of surrender in which I learned I didn't have control over anything, this stage taught me that God does control everything. He demonstrated his ability to provide, and the effect was a powerful impact on my faith.

After several years of working as a consultant, I was offered an opportunity with Mattress Firm. I accepted a position in Houston, and our family packed up and relocated from Atlanta. I had never expected to land in Houston, but I believe it was where God wanted us. It was a big change going from being my own boss to working for a corporation, but the challenge was exciting. I had opportunities to share my faith more openly. In some cases, sharing looked like a prayer of encouragement or words of support to coworkers. In other cases, a few coworkers surrendered their lives to Jesus.

God moved me out of my comfort zone and prompted me to be bold. I remember the influence of 2 Timothy 1:7 on my heart: "For God has not given us a spirit of fear and timidity, but of power, love, and self-discipline." A spirit of power. A spirit of love. A spirit of self-discipline. These traits rolled around in my head and my heart and proved to be very convicting. This season of work solidified my commitment to share my faith openly and let the name of Jesus be known every chance I got. Over time, I had many chances to share, and I am so grateful for the work I was given to do.

In early 2017, after I had transitioned to a new role in the company, we reorganized some of the reporting structure. Unfortunately, the set up didn't work well for me, and I found myself at a fork in the road. Although the company presented me with a very good opportunity to move into a different role, I realized it was time to move on to a new season of work. Once again, God was using this new season to shape a part of my faith that had never been very strong. He was teaching me how to wait for him.

As new work opportunities came along, I committed first to pray and seek God's plan for my life. In many cases, God was quiet, and I waited for a clearer understanding of what to do next. Waiting for anything is hard, but waiting for God is a real challenge for me. God often works in years and decades while I think in terms of minutes, hours, or maybe a day or two. It's scary. But when I read my Bible and consider the work God has done in my life, I rest in his promises that those who wait for him will gain new strength. I like the way that sounds.

There was a time in my life when I looked to my work for significance and meaning. I had a tremendous amount of identity wrapped up in what I did and who I was at work. Fortunately, after I surrendered my life to Jesus, God reshaped my perspective on the purpose of work. Work became less about who I was, and more about what God wanted me to do at work. I had a chance to represent Jesus in a way that could open opportunities to share the message of salvation with the people around me. My identity became who I was as an adopted child of God, and work became a place to share that truth. Every person who surrenders to Jesus has an opportunity to do the same thing!

The Bible says that every follower of Jesus is a priest and part of a royal priesthood (1 Pet. 2:9). My favorite definition of a priest came from my friend Winston: "a person who talks to God about people and talks to people about God." That is who we are in every arena of life, including our workplace. We were each created for a purpose, and work provides a powerful environment for living out that purpose—reflecting characteristics of the God who created us.

2

The State of Work:
God's Way and the World's Way

Many people don't like their jobs. And with the amount of time most spend at work, you can see how frustration and misery can form. I had my own difficult experience at 23 during my first job at a beverage company in Dallas, Texas. I took the job thinking it was going to be a great path toward a career in that industry. The training program was well designed, and my new boss seemed interested in helping me find success. The career path was wide open, and it seemed as though most of the people I met there really enjoyed what they were doing. Out of the gate, it all looked promising.

Ultimately, I settled into my new territory of convenience stores and top-level grocery stores. My job was to keep their beverage areas stocked while presenting any new promotional opportunities on our existing collection of beer and wine. Sounds simple enough, and it was, until I actually made my first big sale. A grocery store decided to purchase one hundred cases of one of our premier wines in order to build a holiday display at the front of the store. I could not have been more excited. That excitement quickly faded when my boss told me I was the one who would need to build the display. On top of that, the store had a policy that displays could not be built during regular shopping hours. They were gracious enough to allow me to come after 9:00 pm. Boy was I . . . excited.

Not really. As you can imagine, I was both frustrated and a little exasperated. I made it back to the store that night, following a full day of work, and assembled the display. By 2 a.m., it was done. It was somewhat extravagant, but it displayed all one hundred cases with a nice golf theme to support the 4th of July holiday. Mission accomplished. But I was exhausted, and had begun to doubt this newfound career path.

Several months later, I sold another large purchase to a convenience store. This time there was no display to build, so the after-hours work session was off the table. The order would arrive on a Friday, and if all went well, the store would sell most of it over the course of the weekend. Unfortunately, there was a problem with shipping, and the order arrived much later than anticipated. Our operations team had a plan B, which required me to help unload the order so that the workers could finish before the receiving dock closed for the day. There I was in my business pants, button-down shirt, and tie unloading cases of beverages in the Texas July heat. I'll never forget that day. Three hours of running boxes from the back of the truck across the black top and into the back of the store was awful. I remember thinking to myself that this dream job was slowly turning into a nightmare.

The job that had looked so promising at the start had turned out to be terrible, and I finally resigned. Why did the work have to be so grueling? Well, I was in my early 20s at the time and had little experience with a real job or an understanding of the nature of work.

The Bible introduces work in the opening chapter, explaining how it began and the way it changed when sin entered the world. In the first verse of the first book of the Bible, we read about work: "In the beginning, God created the heavens and the earth." The Bible begins with highlighting the work God did to create the earth and everything in it. The entire first chapter of Genesis is a play-by-play of creation: the light, day and night, then the dry lands and the sea, followed by plants, vegetation, living creatures, and finally man. The chapter wraps up with God charging man to go to work: "*Be fruitful and multiply, and fill the earth, and subdue it; and rule over the fish of the sea and over the birds of the sky and over every living thing that moves on the earth*" (Gen. 1:28). Be fruitful, multiply, subdue the earth, rule over—all these things sound like work. Work is defined as "exertion or effort directed to *produce or accomplish something*; labor; toil" (emphasis added).[1] God was bringing life into existence for his purpose and his pleasure (Rev. 4:11).

In the early chapters of Genesis, we get a glimpse of God's approach to work. Every time he spoke, something came to be. Ultimately, we see how God operated as he finished up his work. In Genesis 2:2, we read, "*By the seventh day God completed His work which He had done, and He rested on the seventh day from all His work which He had done.*" God completed the work and rested. Work was part of God's perfect design, because he intended us to tend to his creation. Man was given the responsibility to look after what God had done *before* sin entered the world, before the serpent tempted Eve at the Tree of the Knowledge of Good and Evil. When everything was in unity and perfect, work was part of the plan, and it was good.

Unfortunately, if you know the story, you know what's next. Although the Bible doesn't clearly cover how work was done prior to sin, I think it's safe to assume it wasn't hard labor. Then sin happened, and everything changed. The Genesis account after Adam and Eve disobeyed God records the curse in chapter 3. Read these words nice and slow, making note of everything that changes:

Then to Adam He said, "Because you have listened to the voice of your wife and have eaten from the tree about which I commanded you, saying, 'You shall not eat from it'; cursed is the ground because of you; in toil you will eat of it all the days of your life. Both thorns and thistles it shall grow for you; And you will eat the plants of the field; By the sweat of your face You will eat bread, till you return to the ground, because from it you were taken; For you are dust, and to dust you shall return."

—Gen. 3:17–19

The world of work went from perfection and unity with God to an obstacle-filled and grueling activity because of sin. We were created for work from the beginning, but sin changed the nature of it. Now it was going to be difficult.

If you've ever been a farmer or know any farmers, you can understand what this change means. Work is tiresome and grueling. The ground grows thorns and thistles, obstacles to abundant growth. By sweat and labor, man must work until he dies. That's a bit of a sobering description. In a few short sentences, God proclaims what is true about our work today. It is difficult, filled with obstacles, but we are still charged to do it.

The world of work is still difficult, filled with obstacles and often grueling. Don't get me wrong: there are many people who love what they do. But I think in moments of candor and transparency, most people will admit there are times when work absolutely feels like what it is—work! The paradigm of work shifted dramatically after Adam and Eve sinned, and we are all faced with living in light of that shift. Despite the unfortunate addition of pain and suffering, God still commands us to work, and he can use our work as a powerful platform for his message. Unfortunately, many of us don't see work for the opportunity it is. In fact, many people see work as a burden and a necessary evil.

In March 2017, CBS News published an article entitled, "Why So Many Americans Hate Their Jobs." The main point of the article highlighted a recent Gallup study on the American workplace, noting that "two-thirds of American workers are disengaged to some degree at work."[2] That means almost seven out of ten people in *your* office are likely to feel no real connection to their job. In some cases, they may be showing up simply to collect the paycheck. Being disengaged in your job will make it difficult to see the opportunity to live your faith in your workplace.

The CBS article went on to note a few more shocking statistics[3]:

1. 51% of American workers say they are "definitely not engaged."
2. One out of three American workers are millennials, and this group has different expectations than previous generations, including a greater demand on purpose-filled work places.
3. 16% of American workers are "actively disengaged" at work. This means they resent their jobs, tend to gripe to coworkers, and drag down morale as a result.

The impact of being disengaged and lacking purpose is significant. The CBS article also notes, "Companies with lots of unhappy employees pay a price in terms of absenteeism, turnover, productivity, customer service, and even internal theft, otherwise known as shrinkage."[4] Disengaged people cost companies money and have a negative impact on people around them. And, if they are Christians, they significantly limit their availability to be used by God in the workplace.

A disengaged employee is someone who doesn't enjoy work, does the bare minimum, doesn't put in extra effort when needed, and is highly unlikely to have anything positive to say about the company. Although this is a broad description, it offers a simple point of comparison to what the Bible teaches us regarding God working through us.

The Bible says to "*count it **all** joy, my brothers when you meet trials of various kinds*" (James 1:2 ESV, emphasis added). Joy is a hallmark of the follower of Jesus. James later explains that joy can be present no matter your circumstances. Joy can't mean constant happiness, because that's not possible. However, I do think that joy is something we choose. For the follower of Jesus, the ability to choose joy in every circumstance is found in the fact that there is life beyond the one we are living today. We will absolutely experience difficult times, but knowing that God is good and promises an eternity free from pain and suffering helps to put life's challenges into perspective. If you're disengaged in your job, reflecting joy is going to be a major challenge.

The Bible also tells us, "*Show yourself in all respects to be a model of good works, and in your teaching show integrity [and] dignity*" (Titus 2:7 ESV). Disengaged people are the opposite of a model for good works. Although the product of their work may be acceptable to the job description, others see more than the work. People around us see how we speak about our company, our coworkers, and the leaders of our organizations. They see how much, or how little, we follow the policies and procedures of our company. Disengaged people will undermine their potential to be used by God because of the negative impact they make on those around them.

The Bible also makes this powerful point about Jesus: "*Now all glory to God, who is able, through his mighty power at work within us, to accomplish infinitely more than we might ask or think*" (Eph. 3:20 ESV). Jesus was an above-and-beyond person. When it came to loving people, he taught that if someone asks you for a coat, give him two. He encouraged his followers to do more than they thought they could, because that is what he did for each one of us. Jesus didn't take shortcuts; he didn't compromise his integrity. He went out of his way to personally connect with people. If going above and beyond is more than you're willing to do in your workplace, then it will be challenging for you to impact others with your faith.

Finally, consider what Paul wrote in Ephesians 2:10: "*For we are His workmanship, created in Christ Jesus for good works, which God prepared beforehand so that we would walk in them.*" We are each created to work, and the workplace is one of the more visible places to do the job God has for us. How can a disengaged and unhappy person reflect the good works God prepared for them?

Christians have a tremendous opportunity at work. The workplace is filled with people looking for more. This is why the message of Jesus has so much potential to be shared. People are looking for purpose and meaning in their lives, and reflecting a bright light to a darkened workplace offers hope and encouragement. Jesus provided the greatest gift of all time when he suffered for sin in our place, died on the cross, and then rose from the dead. He bridged the insurmountable gap between a holy God and sinful people. Don't let the circumstances of your job prevent you from seeing your workplace as a mission field, a place where you can demonstrate God's design for work and proclaim the truth of Jesus!

3

Work as Worship

When you read the word *worship*, what comes to mind? Do you think about something you are fully invested in? Maybe you think about a Sunday church service and singing songs and hymns. You might consider certain biblical actions as an expression of your devotion to God. Without the truth of the Bible, *worship* can be a misunderstood word. In Romans 12:1, Paul writes, "*Consider your bodies a living and holy sacrifice, acceptable to God, which is your spiritual form of worship.*" He links worship to the sacrifice of our bodies. Said a bit differently, whatever we do with our bodies that honors God can be considered worship. When it comes to work, we typically don't think about it as worship. In most cases, if work and worship are used in the same sentence, people perceive the idea negatively. Unfortunately, too many people worship their work and miss what the Bible says about our work being worship.

"Live to work, or work to live." That's the common mindset in the world today. It assumes that most people fall into one of these two categories.

The live-to-work people are those who place work as their top priority. When deciding where to spend their time and resources, they usually give work their best. Some might even consider this type of person a workaholic. According to *Psychology Today*, work-aholics are constantly thinking of ways to free up more time for work. They often spend much more time working than intended, and they often work in order to reduce feelings of guilt or anxiety.[1] Work helps them feel productive, significant, and alive. A downside of the live-to-work mindset is that these people can easily become stressed if they're hindered from working. I personally don't believe the live-to-work mindset automatically makes you a workaholic, but the line between the two is so fine that it can be a challenge determining when you have crossed over into an unhealthy space. If you are not sure you have crossed over, ask a few people close to you. You might quickly discover that your attitude of, "I just love the work I get to do," has slowly wandered into "work is what is most important to me." If that's the case, it may be time to reevaluate your priorities.

There was a time in my life when I would have identified with the live-to-work group. During my career in the mattress industry, there were very few days that actually felt like work to me. Don't get me wrong: I experienced seasons of high stress, uncertainty, and frustrations at work. But when I look at the big picture over the course of 25 years, I really loved what I was doing. My personal formula for living to work was this: doing work I loved to do with people I loved to do it with. Not a very sophisticated formula, but it sums up my professional experience. We were in the business of helping people sleep better, and it was incredibly rewarding. Unfortunately, the best part of work was sometimes the worst part. It was easy for me to forget about other areas of my life and place all my focus and energy into work. There were times when my job interfered with my family, and that was a problem. I constantly had to resist the temptation to give my work more time than it really required.

The work-to-live folks view work very differently. They go to work because it allows them to do more of the things they like to do outside of work. In some cases, their job provides funds for their hobbies and leisure, while in other cases, a flexible work schedule allows them the freedom to participate in what makes them happy. Unlike their counterparts, the work-to-live group does not spend time thinking about how to work more. Work itself doesn't make them feel more productive or significant. In fact, for this group, they think about their job less so they can spend more time doing what they want to be doing.

I have a friend from college who was the consummate work-to-live person. In fact, he would regularly look for ways to minimize the amount of time he spent with work so that he could spend time sailing his boat, riding his motorcycle, or working out. He showed up right when work started, and left as soon as the workday ended. If there was an opportunity to miss a work-related event, you can be sure he wasn't showing up. When he was at work, the quality of what he did was good, but rarely above and beyond. Over the years, he bounced around from job to job, never really finding a place that allowed him to maximize his own skills and accelerate his career progress. But the truth is, he was never interested in a career path. He worked so he could live.

Which group do you fall into? Are you a work-to-live or live-to-work person? There is a chance you might fall somewhere in the middle. You might view your work as fun and engaging, but given the opportunity, you'd leave it today for a little more money or something more challenging.

What about a third way to view work? What about the idea of work-as-worship? It might seem to be a stretch to call work *worship*, but when you read the Bible, there is clear evidence of this mindset. As the early church was forming, believers were sharing the message of Christ on a daily basis. Many of these early believers spent their days working alongside others to provide for their daily needs; they had plenty of opportunity to share their faith, a faith that fully integrated what they believed with how they lived. What a novel concept.

Before you simply accept work-to-worship as true or not, I would like to make a case for why work can and should be considered worship. I am not an attorney or a very persuasive person, so I am going to let the words of Scripture speak for themselves.

Live As an Example

There are a number of places in the Bible where Jesus teaches righteous living in order to draw others to himself. He illustrates this in Matthew 7:15–17 NLT:

> *"Beware of false prophets who come disguised as harmless sheep but are really vicious wolves. You can identify them by their fruit, that is, by the way they act. Can you pick grapes from thornbushes, or figs from thistles? A good tree produces good fruit, and a bad tree produces bad fruit."*

Basically, watch out for people who say one thing but do another. People are known for what they do and not for what they say.

Earlier in Matthew, Jesus made the point that Christians are a reflection of God:

> *"You are the light of the world. A city set on a hill cannot be hidden; nor does anyone light a lamp and put it under a basket, but on the lampstand, and it gives light to all who are in the house. Let your light shine before men in such a way that they may see your good works and glorify your Father who is in heaven."*

—Matt. 5:14–16

He makes it clear that Christians, because of who they are in Christ, are a light to the rest of the world. I love that example of light because it suggests we are showing a way or helping others to see more clearly, shining Christ's message of repentance and eternal life.

Show the way so that people turn to God. When people see what we do, we reflect what and whom we believe. Actions speak louder than words, and Jesus has called us to be an accurate example of himself and his ways. I find it interesting that there are no conditions or unique circumstances called out around our *"light shining before men in such a way that they may see [our] good works and glorify [our] Father who is in heaven."* My takeaway is that this command applies all the time, no matter where we are, and no matter what we're doing. Given the amount of time spent in the workplace, you can conclude that this challenge applies there as well. Like every other domain of life, what we do at work reflects what we believe.

Our Body As Worship

Our bodies themselves and what we do with them are worship. Earlier I wrote about Romans 12:1, in which the apostle Paul writes, *"Therefore I urge you, brethren, by the mercies of God, to present your bodies a living and holy sacrifice, acceptable to God, which is your spiritual service of worship."* We have an opportunity to worship God by how we live. Our bodies are designed to be a "living and holy sacrifice," which often can be reflected in the form of serving. Serving itself starts in our minds with the willingness to serve, but until we do something, serving is just a nice thought. Considering how much time your physical body spends at work, it's no wonder the workplace offers such a powerful platform for worship.

Many Christians serve others in their church or community. The church has been on the front-end of service for centuries. But what about applying that same practice in your workplace? Unfortunately, I have seen my share of professing Christ-followers decline invitations to help others at work in the interest of getting to their small group meeting or the local soup kitchen. Don't get me wrong, small group time and serving people in need honor God and are part of a solid worship life with Jesus. But what opportunities are we missing by not applying that same mindset at work? I struggled in this area, and I believe I missed out on a number of opportunities to reflect Jesus with my coworkers.

When I worked at Mattress Firm, we supported foster children from a philanthropic perspective. The organization was dedicated to improving the lives of kids who desperately needed the help. As a result, there were often fund-raising events or collection drives designed to provide aid wherever possible. The problem was that many of these events were on weekends or in the evenings, so I often declined to attend. I reasoned that I put in plenty of time with the company during the week, so anything more on the weekend was cutting into either family, church, or small group time. However, as I reflect on those opportunities, I can't help but think I missed out on sharing my faith in Jesus more frequently. Regardless of someone's personal beliefs, serving at an event to help foster children typically opened up doors to talk about topics beyond the day-to-day work conversations. If I had seen the potential in participating to actively serve with my coworkers, who knows what doors God may have opened for a conversation about things of faith.

The way we do our work is powerfully connected to our worship. The words we speak reveal a lot about who we are on the inside. The way we deal with people reflects our true character; the way we use our hands and feet highlights what we really value.

How do you do your work? Do you work to serve your own interests, or the interests of others? Is your work about individual achievement through promotion or recognition? Are you working to accumulate enough money so that you don't have to work in the future? The world around us says that work is where you can find significance and meaning for your life. It says that the more you earn, the more successful you have become. It says that once you have accumulated enough money to retire, then you can live the easy life, doing the things you want to do instead of what you have to do. But the Bible doesn't support any of those concepts. God designed work to be an arena for worship, a place where we share Jesus with others and look for opportunities to help them grow in their relationship with him.

Jesus himself modeled work when he lived out the ministry God planned for him. He made it clear that he came to earth to do the work the Father gave him to do. In fact, in his last prayer before the crucifixion, Jesus said, "I have glorified You on the earth by completing the work that You gave Me to do" (John 17:4). In Christ's case, the work was complete, and it was time to finish what had been started. Jesus set a powerful example for purpose-filled work. Through it all, he worshipped the Father in his work. For us, work can look the same. It is a place where we are serving, loving, and reflecting the character traits of Jesus. Work is worship.

4

Showing Faith before Sharing Faith

Modern Christianity spends lots of time emphasizing certain commands presented in the Bible. One of the more popular points of emphasis is evangelism, sharing the good news of Jesus with others. When you hear the word *evangelism*, what picture comes to mind? Do you instantly think about a recent Sunday school class where the instructor walked you through the top methods of sharing your faith with others? Do you think about the pastor going door-to-door, asking people if they've made a decision for Jesus? Maybe you picture a Christian talking to friends or family who have not yet decided to follow Jesus. Whatever comes to mind, one thing is likely true: the idea of evangelism can be much easier to talk about than it is to do. For many followers of Jesus, this single word brings about a variety of emotions that can stand in the way of living our faith at work.

A number of years ago, I watched a television series on NBC called *Fear Factor*. The show pits contestants against each other in a variety of stunts for a grand prize of 50 thousand dollars. As you can imagine, many people wanted to get into the competition and try their hand at winning the jackpot. For any competitive person, this opportunity might sound like an exciting way to spend an evening. But there was a catch. The "stunts" were created by professionals and often extremely dangerous.

Usually, the first stunt tested the physical abilities of participants. For example, they might have to jump from one building to another or hang from a helicopter collecting flags. It was intense. The second stunt was a mental challenge that pressed the boundaries of common sense and, in my opinion, safety. I remember one episode where a contestant climbed into a box and was covered in non-venomous snakes. That's right: covered in snakes. They had to remain in the box for a period of time before they could exit. Finally, those who were still in the competition (I would have dropped out at snakes) had to participate in some type of extreme stunt you might find in an action movie. It usually involved high-risk speeds, mind-bending heights, or some other kind of over-the-top challenge to test the resolve of the contestants. If you survived, you were crowned the winner. It was one of the most extreme game challenges a person could ever encounter. However, I bet if I asked you to share your faith at work, you might consider *Fear Factor* less intimidating. For some reason, the topic of faith at work stirs up fear and uncertainty. Why is the topic such a scary one?

It starts with the fact that Christians don't think they know how to share their faith. Add to that the pressure in many workplaces to leave your faith at Sunday church, and you have the perfect combination of fear and resistance. But I think that more than ever, we need to bring our entire self, including our faith, to the workplace in a way that honors God and encourages the people in our circle of influence. It's a great win-win opportunity. It's also an opportunity that, if pursued incorrectly, can frustrate and alienate the people around us. Discovering the best way to do it is an important step every Christian should take.

My suggestion is to first *show* your faith before you ever consider *sharing* it. This means living your life in a way that reflects the characteristics of Jesus—honesty, love, compassion, and a willingness to serve others while expecting nothing in return. If Christians are willing to consider how they can first reflect Jesus, there will be plenty of opportunities to talk about him. St. Francis of Assisi once said, "Preach the gospel at all times. When necessary, use words." Each of us can move from fearful to fearless by first demonstrating our faith by the way we live.

The people around us notice our actions and attitudes. People pay attention to what we do, as well as what we don't do. Our reputation at work can influence our impact in the lives of others. No matter how often you say the right things, what you do speaks louder. Our actions speak volumes about what we believe.

Shortly after we opened our first Mattress Firm store locations, the original founders of the company sold the business to a private equity firm. As a result, the senior leadership changed immediately. We were now working with a completely new set of people, only this time, the new team was a group of professing Christians. They even used one of the books of the Bible as the name for their organization. They were front and center with their faith. The problem was that they were front and center with talking about their faith, but not so much living it during the course of daily business.

The highlight of this one-sided approach was the year their president and CEO decided to record a Christmas video in which he presented the story of the birth of Jesus. The point of the message was that Jesus was the reason for the season. Up to that point, I could see the motivation behind the production. However, things went a little sideways when the video was distributed to the entire organization, including the independently owned and operated franchise group. Everyone was directed to show the video to their local teams. It wasn't a request or a suggestion, but a mandatory requirement. Regardless of what we thought about Christmas and the belief systems of our various groups, we were told to show the corporate video. We chose not to show it because we weren't comfortable with the method being used to push a message like this to the company.

I realize that a video highlighting the story of Jesus's birth isn't a confrontational message. In fact, now that I am a follower of Jesus, I couldn't agree more with the need to point people to Jesus. However, I wasn't a believer at the time, and neither were most of the people on our team. It was insulting to be directed to show something to our group that didn't line up with where we were in our faith.

Years later, as I reflect on my own approach to sharing Jesus and the examples I have seen from others, I know there is a better way. In fact, I think there are three arenas we must navigate well to most effectively show our faith to others. The first is the words we use, followed by the integrity we show, and finally, the way we treat people.

1. The Words We Use

Unfortunately, one of the downsides of faith at work is that professing Christians can undermine their ability to share their faith by how they conduct themselves. This is especially prevalent when people express anger or frustration, or when they value profit more than people. The opportunity to show others what Jesus looks like is compromised if we live our lives contradictory to what he teaches.

Shortly after I started a new job, I had the opportunity to reconnect with a friend from college. He'd been working at the same company for a number of years, so I was excited to reconnect and ask him for help in getting up to speed on the priorities of the business. We had a chance to catch up on family, friends, and, to my excitement, faith. He was sharing his own faith story, and I was excited to learn he had surrendered his life to Jesus. What an excellent opportunity to find another person excited about sharing the story of Jesus with others! We had a great time except for one nagging part of our conversation. My friend used a lot of profanity when describing some of the challenges the organization was facing. This wasn't the periodic swear word, but a constant use of expletives that made it challenging for me to follow him. I could relate to his passion and commitment to the company, but the way he expressed himself was hard to understand. How could someone professing to follow Jesus communicate in a way that is opposite what the Bible teaches? I couldn't help but wonder what impact it had on his personal testimony. Eventually, I learned that his communication style almost completely nullified his testimony. As I got to know more people on the team, I could see their perception of my friend was anchored in his intense use of profanity. He had professed one thing but reflected another.

The way we talk to others reflects what we believe. The apostle Paul addressed the language issue in Ephesians 4:29: *"Let no unwholesome word proceed from your mouth, but only such a word as is good for edification according to the need of the moment, so that it will give grace to those who hear."* There are countless situations and events that will escalate your blood pressure and test your patience. In many cases these situations can ignite powerful emotions that need to be expressed, but the Bible challenges us to not let those moments result in using foul language. We are encouraged to hold back unwholesome words and use our speech to edify. The word *edify* means: to build up, encourage, and correct.[1] These verses don't tell us to pretend the situation didn't occur, but they do tell us to speak with correction and edification. If you profess Jesus, the language you use matters, for it can empower your testimony, or undermine everything you hope to accomplish. Please choose your words wisely.

2. The Integrity We Show

Another stumbling block that can undermine an accurate reflection of Jesus is integrity—or rather, the lack thereof.

In 2015, I was honored to receive the Spirit of Life award at the Mattress Firm annual leadership conference. This award was especially meaningful because it recognizes a single individual who exemplifies the heart and spirit of the principles the company was founded on in 1986. Past honorees serve as a "who's who" in the history of the company. It's the equivalent of being selected to the hall of fame in the world of sports, although clearly not as high-profile.

The thing I remember the most was the CEO's opening line. As he spoke, I had no idea he was about to announce my name. He said, "This year's winner is a person who has demonstrated a tremendous track record of integrity." A tremendous track record of integrity. Me. I remember that moment so vividly because prior to knowing Jesus, I don't think a "track record of integrity" would have been my label.

I knew the number of times I either omitted the full truth or exaggerated the specifics of a situation to gain an advantage. The time I charged expenses to the business that were likely more personal than work related. The negotiations where I rounded the financial data in my favor to prove a point and gain an advantage. The interview when I exaggerated the earnings potential to a new candidate to make the job more attractive. Many of those situations could be easily explained, and maybe even justified, but I knew I compromised my integrity.

Although being recognized as someone with integrity was an honor, I felt a bit like a fraud. I knew when and where I had compromised. My outward appearance of integrity may have looked neat and clean, but my heart wrestled with doing right on a regular basis. Thankfully, the principles Jesus taught provide a clearer picture of how he wants me to live. When you consider your own commitment to integrity, are you guided by your heart, or the truth taught in God's word?

Integrity is the quality of honesty and "adherence to moral and ethical principles."[2] But what are strong moral principles? I believe most everyone has moral principles, but are they the right ones? What makes one person's moral principle another person's moral compromise? There are countless books written on this topic. But I want to look at two simple principles the Bible teaches that have guided my own journey toward God's standards for integrity.

The first is in Psalm 15:4a NLT: "And keep their promises even when it hurts." As I thought about the idea of not changing and keeping my promises, even if it hurts, I became convicted to apply it in my life. Prior to that, when something didn't go as planned, I was a mastermind at adjusting, justifying, or modifying how to respond. In consideration of God's standard, I realized I needed to change. Making promises and honoring them no matter the cost is easy to say, but not easy to practice. I will spend most of my life fine-tuning this practice and regularly picking myself up when I fall down.

The second Bible verse that has had a powerful impact on me is John 8:32: *"And you will know the truth, and the truth will make you free."* There is freedom in truth. I know this because I've experienced my fair share of captivity through lying. You know the drill. You bend the truth on one thing, only to find you need to continue to bend the truth as long as the situation is present in your life. Parents tell their children that lies create more lies, but we grow up forgetting those words of wisdom and dabbling in compromises that often produce more compromises. Choosing the truth sets you free and keeps you free.

3. The Way We Treat People

A third way we can more accurately reflect a picture of our faith at work is how we treat others. If you have been a Christian for any length of time, you won't be wowed by that statement. In fact, you don't have to have any foundation in faith to acknowledge that truth. Society often holds up the golden rule as the standard for dealing with people—and not the golden rule that says, "He who has the most gold, rules." I am talking about the one that says, "Do unto others as you would have them do unto you." Treat people the way you want to be treated. Show people the same courtesy, care, and consideration you would want them to show you. This rule is easily understood but not always easily applied. It can be particularly challenging in the workplace. For some reason, in many work environments, people decide to set their Sunday morning kindness and gentleness aside and replace it with aggression and self-interest. If you profess Jesus as Lord, then reflecting those character traits won't work.

Unfortunately, modern day culture supports the idea of professing Jesus on Sunday but putting others down on Monday. The workplace can be demanding, and the pressure to conform to the world can be subtle and sneaky. But followers of Jesus are commanded to treat people the way Jesus would treat them. There are many verses in the Bible that speak about loving one another, being kind to one another, encouraging one another, and serving one another. Jesus hit the point directly when he said,

"Love your enemies! Do good to them. Lend to them without expecting to be repaid. Then your reward from heaven will be very great, and you will truly be acting as children of the Most High, for he is kind to those who are unthankful and wicked. You must be compassionate, just as your Father is compassionate."

—Luke 6:35–36 NLT

Do you have enemies at work? Love them. Does someone need something? Consider giving it to them. Are some people unkind and difficult? Be kind and accommodating. I realize these statements are easier to write than to apply, but that's what Jesus urges us to do.

Over and over again, Jesus challenged his followers to do what may often seem super-human. Be kind to those who are unkind to you. Love those who persecute you. Give more than what people are asking for, even if they don't intend to pay you back. How in the world is someone supposed to live this way? Well, Jesus also explains that, on our own, these things are impossible. It's only with him that *everything* is possible. Trusting Jesus is an important part of reflecting our faith.

As we surrender more of our own desires and selfish ways to Jesus, our trust increases. Understanding what the Bible says and applying it in our daily lives also builds trust. One of the more profound ways to gain a deeper understanding of God's word is reframing Bible verses. This technique involves restating Bible verses in the opposite way they're written. I actually learned the idea of "opposites" years ago from a friend named Chic Thompson. Chic is an author, speaker, and teacher who specializes in creativity. He designed the process of thinking in opposites to help individuals and groups improve their creative capabilities. When it comes to God's word, this technique has helped me gain a deeper understanding of how to apply what I read. Let me give you a few examples from verses we covered earlier in this chapter.

What we say matters, and Ephesians 4:29 provides guidance on how to think about our words: "Let no unwholesome word proceed from your mouth, but only such a word as is good for edification according to the need of the moment, so that it will give grace to those who hear." An opposite approach on this verse might read something like this: "*Let unwholesome words come out of your mouth, and only words that aren't encouraging in the current situation and that give grace to no one.*" You won't give grace to anyone. That statement catches my attention and challenges me even more to consider the importance of my words and how they impact others.

Another verse I referenced earlier was John 8:32: "*And you will know the truth, and the truth will make you free.*" The opposite of that verse might read, "And you will only know lies, and the lies make you a prisoner all your life." Lies will keep you in prison, in bondage. I don't know about you, but I have no interest in a life characterized by bondage. That thought pushes me toward a desire to know as much truth as I can.

Previously, I included Jesus's words in Luke 6:35–36:

"Love your enemies! Do good to them. Lend to them without expecting to be repaid. Then your reward from heaven will be very great, and you will truly be acting as children of the Most High, for he is kind to those who are unthankful and wicked. You must be compassionate, just as your Father is compassionate."

Written in the opposite, it would say, "Don't love your enemies, do bad, don't lend people anything. If you do, make sure you expect something in return. If you live like this, you won't be rewarded, and you won't be a child of God. God is not kind to unthankful and wicked men, and he is not merciful." What a picture that opposite verse paints! It sounds crazy when you read it, but think about it. How many people don't love their enemies? How many people lend to others and always expect something in return? How many of us have trouble giving mercy to the people around us? The idea of not being rewarded and not receiving mercy from God moves me to treat my enemies the way the Bible calls me to treat them.

There is nothing supernatural about reframing Bible verses in opposite language, but this method can provide further depth into what is being said. As we understand God's word more deeply, it equips us to live the way God intended.

The way I speak to and around people at work is part of showing my faith. Making decisions and acting with the highest levels of integrity reflect the standards I've established in my life. How I treat the people around me, even the ones I don't like that much, serves as a profound statement for my true character. How I do each of these reflects my beliefs, and ultimately, whom I believe in. It's a blessing to have an opportunity to share faith with someone at work, but if we start with showing it, then the opportunities to share will take care of themselves.

5

Purposeful Prayer

Prayer is one of the foundational topics of the Christian faith. There have been thousands of books written on it, and tens of thousands of messages preached on it. But how many people bring prayer to their workplace? If you work in an environment where prayer is permitted, do you regularly call upon God throughout your day? Do you work in a place where prayer is frowned upon? If so, how often do you pray in the quiet of your heart at work? More often I find that many have great intentions to pray, but they miss out on the opportunities to do it. I have found myself frustrated when I come to the end of the day and realize I didn't stop at all to pray.

The truth is that our opportunity to impact others in the workplace will be limited if we don't ask Jesus to be part of what we are doing on a daily basis. Don't get me wrong: God can exercise his power and authority wherever and whenever he chooses. But he has invited us to ask anything in his name, and he will do it (John 14:14). How often are you talking to God about the details of your day at work? Have you ever offered to pray for someone in the moment right as they shared a challenging circumstance or story with you? If we take that step, God will work powerfully and directly in the workplace with his people.

I realize that prayer at work is not always a natural thing to do. I remember a colleague who told me about a terrible visit he and his wife had at the doctor's office. His wife was diagnosed with a life-threatening illness, and they were concerned about the future. I asked if I could pray for them, and he agreed. Unfortunately, I meant to pray right then, and he thought I would do it later. As I bowed my head to pray, he awkwardly stopped me and said, "Not right now." To make an awkward situation worse, I slowly wandered back to my office, and he went back to his, without another word. So much for prayer at the office.

Reflecting on that experience, I am actually grateful for the way it played out. It taught me to offer prayer in the moment. In the event someone reacts negatively to the invitation, then we always have a chance to either pray quietly or pray later. The point is that Jesus says to call on his name. The offer to pray for someone or with someone can be done politely and directly, provided we respond in a way that honors their reaction (aka don't slink awkwardly back to your office). Simply offering to pray demonstrates whom you follow and what is important in your life. Be ready, be willing, and be comfortable to make an offer to pray whenever the opportunity shows itself.

Being purposeful with prayer is an important step in allowing God to use you in the workplace. Commit to praying for the salvation of people in your workplace, for those suffering or scared right when they share their story, and for an open heart and eyes to see who needs prayer and to act on the spot. Being purposeful with prayer at work can bring a sharper focus to an important part of our relationship with Jesus—the part where we simply talk to him. Are you purposeful in what you pray throughout the day?

When I surrendered my life to Jesus, I met a man named Winston who began to disciple me. The relationship looked a lot like a traditional mentoring relationship in that we met regularly to discuss life. He was further down the road than I was in maturity and experience, so he offered advice and challenged me with questions.

The biggest difference in this relationship versus others I had over the course of my career was that this man pointed me to the Bible for wisdom. He rarely, if ever, gave his own opinion. If we were talking through a big decision I was facing, he suggested taking a look at Proverbs 16:3: "*Commit your works to the Lord and your plans will be established.*" I applied the verse by listing out the considerations for my decision and spending time prayerfully committing these things to God, asking him to provide a clear path. It was during our time together that I learned the importance of the question, "What does the Bible say about this?"

As Winston and I spent more time together, he eventually invited me to a luncheon at the local country club in Phoenix. It was a business lunch group that frequently brought in speakers to share their business stories and lessons from their lives. Only in this case, the speakers always shared their stories of surrendering their lives to Jesus and the change it brought in their lives. It was a powerful platform where people could hear the message of Jesus and create an opportunity for discussion. Winston encouraged me to pray for specific people in my circle of influence to bring to the lunch. Most of the people I spent my time with were at work, so I made my list. I prayed that God would change the hearts of five specific people in our company. I had no idea what God had planned. If I had, I don't think my mind could have comprehended it.

The first person on my list was my business partner because we spent a tremendous amount of time together. He also started asking me questions about what I did with Winston when we would meet every Friday. He was curious, so I kept praying God would present more opportunity. Eventually, he accepted an invitation to the lunch, and he even scheduled time to meet with my mentor. Not long afterward, he recommitted his life to Jesus and brought his faith to the workplace. God was working in his heart and a few other hearts as well.

Over the course of a year or so, my brother-in-law surrendered his life to Jesus, followed by my sister. Shortly around that time, one of our top leaders and his wife also surrendered their lives to Jesus. In a crazy case of God working through many people and in many ways, one of our store managers surrendered his life to Jesus when a customer shared the good news of the gospel. One person after another turned to Jesus during this time. God was answering prayers, and our team began to change.

The complicated part of that entire time was that our business was rapidly collapsing. We ran into all kinds of financial trouble and were unable to sustain the rapid growth path we had been on. Over the course of a few years, as people were coming to faith in Jesus, our business was falling apart, and we ultimately sold the company to another operator. I am leaving out a lot of the details, but they really wouldn't help with highlighting the power of prayer. When I look back on it, God was working.

Praying for others at work is one way to invite God more fully into your life, Monday through Friday. But purposeful prayer also offers tremendous potential to make personal requests of God. Going to God before the work day begins and praying for access and influence with others is a great place to start. Asking him to provide you with a grace-filled heart to be his servant for the day honors God. In Ephesians 3:20, Paul writes, *"Now to Him who is able to do far more abundantly beyond all that we ask or think, according to the power that works within us."* Paul is referencing Jesus, who is reminding us he can do even more than we can imagine. Through prayer, we can boldly call on Jesus to be part of our workday and to open doors of opportunity where it might seem challenging. Wherever we see the potential for supernatural help, remember it is available when we ask God directly.

When my business partner and I had our retail stores, we held fellowship times. Before you think that we must have been super

committed to Jesus, I should tell you that our version of fellowship
and the Christian version were pretty different. At the time, we were
not followers of Jesus, so fellowship meant showing up to work early,
heading to the back of the warehouse, putting in a pinch of Skoal
(please don't judge), and talking about the state of the business.
Most of the time our conversations gravitated toward the problems
we were facing: difficult customers we needed to call back, challenging employees we needed to meet with, and demanding suppliers
who wanted more of our business. In hindsight, it was a complaint
session to unload our stress and then encourage each other to get
back after it. One of the things we used to say (sort of) half-jokingly
was, "Business would be so much fun if it wasn't for customers and
employees." We didn't actually believe this, but it helped us escape
the pressures of a growing business.

Despite our appreciation for our customers and our amazing
group of employees, dealing with people can be a challenge. If you
think about it, most of the conflict, tension, and disappointment we
experience in the workplace are connected to people. Dealing with
people in a Christ-like way takes patience, gentleness, understanding,
compassion, and many other characteristics that don't always come
naturally to many people. Prayer offers direct access to the God who
can supply everything we need to not only help us deal with people
but also to create a new heart in each of us. Turning to God makes
dealing with people much easier over time.

Have you asked God to make you different? How can God's perspective of people help you reflect your faith at work in a more accurate and influential way? Hebrews 4:16 says, *"Therefore let us draw
near with confidence to the throne of grace, so that we may receive mercy
and find grace to help in time of need."* We can approach God directly
and access his grace when we need it. Grace is a powerful catalyst
for dealing with people in a way that Jesus would deal with them. If
we can lead with grace, then our hearts can be changed. When we

see people the way God sees them, our hearts change. Purposefully pray that God would give you his eyes, ears, heart, hands, and feet to live your faith in a visible way. This includes the workplace!

I have met countless people over the years who actively live their faith at work. One of the things this group has in common is their emphasis on prayer. Specifically, they pray for people, by name, in their workplace, asking God for grace to love them the way he calls us to love them. We can take every step possible to share the message of Jesus with people at work. We can look for chances to invite people to church or to some other event where faith will be featured. But the unwavering commitment to prayer invites the full power of God into the process. It acknowledges that apart from God, we really can't do anything. I want to encourage you to start living your faith at work through prayer. God can do amazing work when we step aside and submit ourselves to him.

6

Lead with Love

There was a time when I thought the words *love* and *work* would never be used in the same sentence. I believed business was built on intense competition, boot-strapping operating methods, and a commitment to winning. I finished college and transitioned into the business world in the early 1990s. During that time, several of the largest corporate layoffs in the history of business occurred. Terms like *downsizing*, *rightsizing*, and other fancy phrases for letting people go created a work environment that lacked trust. For years there was a bit of *us* versus *them* feeling in many organizations. Over time, this tone has been shifting. Whether you credit the massive expansion of small businesses or the shifting attitudes of the population, turns out the apostle Paul had it right when he wrote about love in I Corinthians 13:1–3 NLT:

> *"If I could speak all the languages of earth and of angels, but didn't love others, I would only be a noisy gong or a clanging cymbal. If I had the gift of prophecy, and if I understood all of God's secret plans and possessed all knowledge, and if I had such faith that I could move mountains, but didn't love others, I would be nothing. If I gave everything I have to the poor and even sacrificed my body, I could boast about it; but if I didn't love others, I would have gained nothing."*

His point is pretty clear: if I don't have love, nothing else matters.

When it comes to sharing your faith with others, leading with love is an important place to begin. This doesn't necessarily mean using the word *love*, but it does mean dealing with people in a loving and caring way. This can look different in every workplace and with every person. The Bible tells us that people will know us by our love. If you want to be effective with your faith at work, then love is key.

If you're a bit skeptical of love at work and don't completely buy into what the Bible says about love, consider an article by Sigal Barsade and Olivia A. O'Neill titled, "Employees Who Feel Love Perform Better." In their initial study, the researchers surveyed employees, patients, and patient families at a long-term healthcare facility and hospital in the Northeast. Their findings illustrated how important emotional culture is to employee and client well-being and performance. They wrote,

> *"Employees who felt they worked in a loving, caring culture reported higher levels of satisfaction and teamwork. They showed up to work more often. Our research also demonstrated that this type of culture related directly to client outcomes, including improved patient mood, quality of life, satisfaction, and fewer trips to the ER."*[1]

Given that the study was done in the healthcare field, which may be more biased toward the emotional, they conducted a follow-up survey across multiple industries only to discover similar results. People who work in environments where they can express affection, care for others, and practice compassion are more engaged and perform better at work.

The researchers used the term "companionate love" to make the point that they are not talking "romantic love" or a love that might be considered inappropriate for the workplace. They defined "companionate love" as something based on warmth, appropriate affection, and connection. I think about it as the love I have for my sister. The Bible would call this love "*brotherly love*" (Heb. 13:1). In Romans 12:10, Paul tells us to "*be devoted to one another in brotherly love; [giving] preference to one another in honor.*"

The Greek word for this type of love used throughout the Bible is *phileo*—brotherly love. Another way to describe it is "a generous and affectionate love that seeks what's best for another person with no expectations from any act of kindness to be returned." This type of love has nothing to do with passion or a hint of sexual interest. It's why the apostle Paul encouraged Christians to love each other in this way, and it's why this type of love is so effective at work. We all have a desire to be accepted, encouraged, and affirmed.

The article included examples of companies and people who were demonstrating "companionate love" and making an impact. They highlighted Whole Foods Market and PepsiCo, who both have management principles that include the words *love* and *caring* on their websites. They also highlighted Zappos: "Zappos also explicitly focuses on caring as part of its values: 'We are more than a team though . . . we are a family. We watch out for each other, care for each other, and go above and beyond for each other.'"[2] That mindset is attractive to people, and it produces a loyalty difficult to divide. The authors go on to mention Cisco CEO John Chambers, who asked that he be notified within 48 hours if a close member of an employee's family passed away.[3] Organizations see the importance of love as part of their culture, and leaders look for opportunities to show care because they know it makes a difference.

Jesus had this figured out thousands of years ago. When we lead with love, we dramatically increase our opportunity to follow up with professing our faith. Jesus said, "*A new commandment I give to you, that you love one another, even as I have loved you, that you also love one another. By this all men will know that you are My disciples, if you have love for one another*" (John 13:34–35). People will know who you are if you show love for one another. Jesus clearly states that the way we love one another will have a powerful impact on the way others see our faith.

The Bible defines love in 1 Corinthians 13:4–6:

"Love is patient, love is kind. It does not envy, it does not boast, it is not proud. It does not dishonor others, it is not self-seeking, it is not easily angered, it keeps no record of wrongs. Love does not delight in evil but rejoices with the truth. It always protects, always trusts, always hopes, always perseveres."

If you are wondering what love at work looks like, here it is. Love looks like this at work, at home, with those closest to us, and with new acquaintances. This definition of love found in the Bible is applicable in all circumstances and with all people. It serves as a powerful roadmap for leading with love wherever we are living.

Love Is Patient and Kind

Are you known as a patient and kind person at work? Do you *want* to be patient and kind at work? The intention of your heart is critical for living a life surrendered to Jesus—if patience and kindness aren't part of your character at work, you will have a difficult time leading with love.

I wrestled with both of these character traits early in my Christian faith. I wasn't patient, and impatience normally kept me from being kind. I don't think the people who knew me best would consider me unkind, but I don't think I would be known for kindness. I was known for getting things done. I was all about business and focusing on what needed to happen to keep things moving forward. If there were some personal challenges in my team, I was normally one of the last to find out. I don't think it was that no one wanted to tell me, but that I had an inability to listen. I was caught up in the work, and I didn't always pick up anything else. That made it tough to lead with love.

Love Does Not Envy or Boast and Is Not Proud

The workplace is a breeding ground for envy, boasting, and pride. In fact, you could argue that pride and a desire to win are important motivators if you want to get ahead. I agree, if getting ahead, anchoring your significance in what you do, and valuing production at work are the standards by which you measure yourself. But those are not the ways God measures us. Jeremiah 9:24 says, *"But let him who boasts boast of this, that he understands and knows Me, that I am the Lord who exercises lovingkindness, justice and righteousness on earth; for I delight in these things, declares the Lord."* Knowing and understanding the Lord is something we can celebrate. Envy, boasting, and pride will only stand in the way of your knowing God and living your faith at work. Each of these deadly traits will keep you too focused on yourself.

Love Does Not Dishonor and Is Not Self-seeking

How many times have you heard someone sell himself by highlighting the negative attributes of another person? Comparison is at the core of evaluation. Competition is at the heart of the daily operations of business. I worked in a sales organization for years and saw firsthand the positive and negative impact a competitive environment can create. The truth is that we don't have to dishonor others or simply seek our own interests to do well. In fact, the more we seek to encourage others and help them get what they're interested in, the more we will find ourselves achieving our own goals.

Love Keeps No Record of Wrongs

Love doesn't anger easily, and it doesn't keep score. This is a hard truth: if you are prone to anger in the workplace, then you will have a hard time making an impact for Jesus. By nature, the work environment can be stressful and competitive. It can encourage questionable practices, regular compromises in integrity, and downright nasty tactics in the interest of shareholder growth. But that doesn't have to be the case with those who follow Jesus. When we realize that our primary purpose for going to work is to reflect Christ and share his message of salvation, the circumstances that ignite our frustrations diminish. Love helps us see people and situations in a new light. Face it: anger or grudges kill your ability to share your faith at work, though they're easy traps to fall into. But when you realize God is in control and wants the best for you, it's easier to lead with love.

Shortly after I was promoted to executive vice president of merchandising, two other colleagues were promoted to EVP levels of their respective departments. The three of us assumed the daily responsibilities of the company. We each reported to the CEO and worked as a group to make sure we were achieving our sales and profit results. I loved both of my counterparts, and working with them was one of the highlights of my career.

Ultimately, our company grew and needed someone to assume the role of chief operating officer. This new role meant that I would either step into it or report to the new person in it. I hoped to get a shot at it, and given my track record, I thought I would be a consideration. Unfortunately, one of my peers was promoted before I could even talk about it. As you can imagine, my initial reaction was a mix of disappointment, frustration, envy, and anger. Why had I not been considered? What could I have done differently to have put myself in a better position for the promotion? For weeks I turned the situation over and over in my mind. It distracted me from my work and stirred up negative feelings about my new boss. Love had left the building, and I was caught in a prison of self-doubt and self-focus. Why me? What did I miss?

Fortunately, I was spending time in my Bible, trying to understand what happened and looking for encouragement in God's word. One morning I came across Psalm 75:6–7, which says, *"For not from the east, nor from the west, nor from the desert comes exaltation; But God is the Judge; He puts down one and exalts another.*" I remember studying this passage several years ago and recalling that the King James Version uses the word *promotion* in place of exaltation. I was instantly convicted. Promotions come from God; he decides when one person is lifted up and another is not. In that moment, I realized that God had complete control over the situation. Peace came over me, and the envy, disappointment, and anger slowly faded. It changed the way I saw the situation and everyone involved, and I found great confidence knowing God had orchestrated the situation. I instantly felt joy for my buddy who had been promoted, and I was looking forward to working with him in a new capacity. God's word changed the way I saw the situation, and my heart changed as a result.

After Paul explains what love isn't, he transitions to what love is. These beautiful illustrations serve as vivid pictures for what God has designed.

Love Rejoices, Protects, and Trusts

Love looks out for other people in a big way. When I read the words *rejoices, protect,* and *trust,* I think of my friend Steve. He served as the CEO of our organization for several years, and no matter the situation, Steve looked out for people on his team. He was trustworthy, and he painted a vision of the future that was always hopeful. In fact, if you think about your favorite boss or someone you have worked with that you respect highly, it is likely they demonstrated several of these traits. Love is looking out for others in a way that builds trust and strengthens commitment to the future. These characteristics can certainly be present in someone who does not have a relationship with Jesus, but when you reflect these, you look different from most people around you. Often, it's in these differences that others become curious about why you do what you do. Bold and forward-facing love is a difference maker.

Love Perseveres

I don't believe it was coincidence that Paul finished up his love statements with the word *perseverance*. When you consider all the other character traits he uses to describe love, you have to wonder how in the world one person can do all those things. The answer is through perseverance and taking it one day, one person, and one situation at a time. One of the most radical differences between the culture's definition of love and the Bible's definition is choice. The world suggests that love is a feeling. The Bible describes love as a choice. We choose to love people and circumstances on a daily basis. Why else would Paul call us to persevere in love? It won't be easy, and we won't always want to do it, but choosing to love is a powerful gift to others. If we stay the course at work and love those who aren't easy to love, we will find more doors opening up to boldly share our faith with others.

These standards may seem high and unreachable. There's a chance that after reading the Bible's summary of what love is and isn't, you could conclude that leading with love is impossible. As you consider the descriptive words Paul wrote against the backdrop of where you are at work, you might feel a sense of defeat. You may be so far from each of these that changing the way you live is the equivalent of turning a butterfly into a dinosaur. But that is exactly what God does when we surrender our lives to Jesus. He gives us a new heart and new desires. There are two important truths to remember about surrendering your life to Jesus.

The first truth is in 2 Corinthians 5:17: "*Therefore if anyone is in Christ, he is a new creature; the old things passed away; behold, new things have come.*" The old things of our lives, including our attitudes and failures, are out; a new way of living is in. We are ready for profound change when we open our lives to be led by Jesus.

The second truth is in Philippians 3:13–14:

"Brethren, I do not regard myself as having laid hold of it yet; but one thing I do: forgetting what lies behind and reaching forward to what lies ahead, I press on toward the goal for the prize of the upward call of God in Christ Jesus."

God is a forward-facing God. The past and its baggage can be unloaded and discarded. Just like Paul, we can forget what lies behind and reach forward to what lies ahead. We can decide to lead with love and watch God honor that decision through opportunities to influence others. If our minds choose it, our hearts will follow, and our work will be more purposeful and more meaningful than ever!

Leading with love in the workplace is not what people expect. Leading with love opens the door for many of the more outward expressions of our faith. Jesus called us first to love him and then to love others as our neighbors. The people we work with everyday are our neighbors, and we are called to love them.

7

Humble at Heart

The idea of leading with love is powerful, but it is difficult to love without humility of the heart. Only in the past decade has humility risen in popularity as a powerful leadership trait, but God knew it long before our culture caught up.

When I entered the workforce in the 1990s, humility was not a celebrated trait. Many of the top business books at the time covered topics like organizational reengineering, improving productivity, and studies on best practices of top companies. The '90s also poked fun at corporate America (e.g., the Dilbert comics). There was very little on the market encouraging leaders to embrace humility. Though humility is a powerful leadership trait, many businesses, which means many people, still struggle to lead with a humble heart. Thankfully, the Bible provides profound insight into humility and how God has used it to significantly impact the lives of his people.

In the Old Testament, God showed Israel their lack of humility and the terrible impact it had on their lives. In the New Testament, Paul writes about its importance over and over again to the early church. In many cases, he leans on Old Testament writings to get to the same conclusion. Humility is essential to the life of a follower of Jesus.

Jesus was the ultimate example of humility. In Philippians 2:5–8, Paul writes,

Have this attitude in yourselves which was also in Christ Jesus, who, although He existed in the form of God, did not regard equality with God a thing to be grasped, but emptied Himself, taking the form of a bond-servant, and being made in the likeness of men. Being found in appearance as a man, He humbled Himself by becoming obedient to the point of death, even death on a cross.

He provides clear instructions to the church: be humble, just as Jesus was humble. We must strive to serve others and live the way God calls us to live in humility. Humility reflects strength and allows a person to be shaped by God rather than their own naturally selfish ways. It is critical for dealing with people. If we can embrace it, we will be in a stronger position to live out our faith in the workplace.

One of my favorite Bible stories on humility in the workplace is the life of Nehemiah, a Jewish man appointed to a high position in the Persian court under King Artaxerxes. He was the king's cup-bearer, a role which gave him direct access to the king. The story opens up with Nehemiah receiving information from his friends about the Jews who had recently returned to Jerusalem. His friends explained that the city was in ruin, it had no walls, and the people were stressed and fearful. During this time, a city without a wall was vulnerable to invasions. Nehemiah knew the tension this could cause, so he was very disturbed by the news. Nehemiah 1:4 describes it this way: "*When I heard these words, I sat down and wept and mourned for days; and I was fasting and praying before the God of heaven.*" Nehemiah then prayed a powerful prayer, asking God for favor in the eyes of the king so that he could start the process of making things right.

After extended prayer and a bold request for a leave of absence, the king allowed Nehemiah to return to Jerusalem to help his people. At every step of the way, Nehemiah prayed first, then took steps toward what he knew was the right thing to do. Humility, or fully depending on God, was at the core of Nehemiah's effort to rebuild the city.

Ultimately, the king appointed Nehemiah provincial governor of the area. Nehemiah started with surveying the damage and developing a plan to address the situation. Notice that he didn't go in with great fanfare or a boldly stated vision. He took a different approach, which demonstrated his humility and complete dependence on God. Nehemiah 2:12 describes his approach: *"And I arose in the night, I and a few men with me. I did not tell anyone what my God was putting into my mind to do for Jerusalem and there was no animal with me except the animal on which I was riding."* Once he understood the situation, he gathered the people to discuss his plan. He told them what God had put in his heart, explained that God had given him favor with the king, and shared his insight on construction. Even in the midst of early opposition, Nehemiah points to God as the one who cleared the way for a successful project.

As the work to rebuild the city gained traction, the other tribes in the area felt threatened. They were concerned that a strong and secure Jewish population would rise up and attack the surrounding groups. These tribes discussed coming together and killing those who were doing the work. When the Jewish people heard the rumors against them, fear spread quickly. However, as a good leader often does, Nehemiah hit this new challenge head-on. He reminded them of the work God had already done up to that point and ended with a simple plan. In Nehemiah 4:14, he says, *"When I saw their fear, I rose and spoke to the nobles, the officials and the rest of the people: 'Do not be afraid of them; remember the Lord who is great and awesome, and fight for your brothers, your sons, your daughters, your wives and your houses.'"* After his speech, the people agreed to arm every worker with a sword and assign a trumpeter to blow the alert if the fight came. Nehemiah acknowledged the fine balance between depending on God but putting an action plan in place to keep the work moving.

As the building project continued, some of the Jewish people became frustrated with the structure of property ownership and the taxes levied on them by the nobles. Once again, Nehemiah's leadership was challenged at work. The people were frustrated and complaining. He had to respond in some way to address the situation and stay focused on rebuilding. In a brilliant move, he appealed to the nobles, pointing out that unnecessary taxes and heavy burdens needed to stop. He made a bold and humble move when he denounced his own access to the food and land allotments entitled to him as governor. In Nehemiah 6:14–15, he writes,

> *Moreover, from the day that I was appointed to be their governor in the land of Judah, from the twentieth year to the thirty-second year of King Artaxerxes, for twelve years, neither I nor my kinsmen have eaten the governor's food allowance. But the former governors who were before me laid burdens on the people and took from them bread and wine besides forty shekels of silver; even their servants domineered the people. But I did not do so because of the fear of God.*

By putting the interests of others above his own and fully trusting God to deliver, Nehemiah could inspire his people to stay the course.

There are a number of other fantastic lessons in leadership, adversity, and reliance on God throughout the book, but the main point is that a humble heart is necessary for living your faith effectively at work. Just as God used Nehemiah to accomplish an amazing revival for his people, he can use each of us to do the same.

When we fully depend on God, we are living with a heart of humility. Just as Nehemiah first turned to God in a difficult situation, so must we when faced with frustration, challenge, or opposition at work. Imagine if the next time you faced a difficult situation, your first step was to seek God's wisdom and guidance. What if you decided to first search the pages of the Bible to see if anyone else has experienced a similar situation? When we seek God first, we immediately shift our focus from ourselves to him. It softens our hearts and opens up our minds to a better way forward.

Nehemiah also demonstrated humility when he first surveyed the situation before acting. How many times have you seen people at work step into a situation and act before gaining a full understanding of the circumstances? This approach often leads to more conflict and frustration and rarely leads to a positive outcome. A humble person realizes there is a lot they don't know and is willing to take the time to learn.

In addition, Nehemiah showed a powerful example of humility when he put other's interests above his own. As governor, he was entitled to certain benefits related to food and land, but when he saw the difficult position the people were in, he forfeited those benefits. People who put the interests of others above their own are humble people.

Although humility is a more celebrated trait in the workplace today, selfishness, narcissism, and greed are still prevalent in many offices. Humility offers a profound way to demonstrate to the world that there is something different in you. It is an attractive difference that often prompts others to ask questions. When they do that, the door is open for you to boldly and directly share your faith.

8

Courageous Conversations

Shortly after the 9/11 terrorist attacks, Allen Kay wanted to help prevent another disaster. As chairman of Korey Kay & Partner's advertising agency in Manhattan, he did what a good ad agency leader would do: he came up with a slogan. The slogan, "If you see something, say something," became a global phenomenon. In a 2010 New York magazine article, Josh Duboff stated that the saying was "the homeland security equivalent of the 'Just Do It' Nike advertisement and has appeared all across the world."[1] If you travel at all, you'll probably see the phrase displayed on a billboard or wall poster. It encourages people to be vigilant as they travel, and report anything that appears potentially harmful. Christians have a similar responsibility to share what we see. Unfortunately, in many work environments, saying something is the very thing we fear.

It's impossible to write about the topic of sharing your faith without referencing the Great Commission that Jesus gave his disciples just before his ascension. He said, "*Go therefore and make disciples of all nations, baptizing them in the name of the Father and the Son and the Holy Spirit, teaching them to observe all that I commanded you; and lo, I am with you always, even to the ends of the age*" (Matt. 28:19–20). We can't make disciples, baptize them, or teach them if we're not speaking up. Unfortunately, too many people start with speaking and forget to humble themselves, lead with love, and be purposeful with prayer. When our heart is in the right place, we can be ready to say something when the opportunity shows up.

I once attended a group business dinner and sat next to a marketing executive at one of our supplier companies. I'd known him through business dealings. Though we'd worked on a few projects together, we never got to know each other personally. But on this particular night, we started asking each other questions about our families, where we grew up, how we got into the industry, and other topics outside of our normal business discussions. At one point, church came up, and I was surprised to learn he was a dedicated churchgoer. Honestly, I was caught off-guard. I never knew he was a Christian—one of my brothers! Then it dawned on me: how many people do I work or interact with on a regular basis who don't know *I'm* a Christian? How many people would be surprised if I shared my faith? I determined that night to do whatever I could in future conversations to bring up faith so that I could quickly determine where the other person was in life and, more importantly, share my own story of faith based on the birth, death, and resurrection of Jesus Christ. I don't want anyone to ever be surprised I am a follower of Jesus.

In previous chapters, we explored the idea of showing faith before sharing faith. It's important that we walk the walk and not just talk the talk, but if we never talk the talk, then we are missing out on an important part of living our faith at work.

Say Something

In Hebrews, we get a clear picture of God's approach in speaking to people: "*God, after He spoke long ago to the fathers in the prophets in many portions and in many ways, in these last days has spoken to us in His Son, whom He appointed heir of all things, through whom also He made the world*" (Heb. 1:1–2). God speaks to us through Jesus, and Jesus himself encourages us to speak to others about repentance and eternal life in him. Saying something about your faith, the reasons you believe what you believe, and what you've discovered as true are all part of being a follower of Jesus.

It's hard to find a better example in the Bible of someone who regularly said something about his faith while working than Daniel. As far as I can tell, he was one of the first to model being a devoted follower of God in a difficult work environment.

If you don't know the story of Daniel, I encourage you to read through the book itself. The first six chapters are particularly helpful, as they cover the first several years of Daniel's career progression and the challenges he faced.

The first real tension begins shortly after Daniel was placed in the king's service as one of his advisors. The king had a dream that disturbed him, and he expected someone from his advisory council to interpret it. After several meetings and discussions, the king realized his men were unable to interpret his dream. In a state of frustration, the king ordered all of his advisors to be killed, or as the text says in Daniel 2:12, he *"gave order to destroy the wise men of Babylon."* Since Daniel was part of this group, he was on the ledger of dead men. But Daniel had a knack for interpreting dreams, so he requested to meet with the king and offer his services. Ultimately, Daniel interpreted the dream, but before giving the meaning to the king, Daniel made it clear that God and God alone was the one who provided him with the skill to interpret dreams. The Bible says it this way in Daniel 2:27–28:

> *"Daniel answered before the king and said, 'As for the mystery about which the king has inquired, neither wise men, conjurers, magicians nor diviners are able to declare it to the king. However, there is a God in heaven who reveals mysteries, and He has made known to King Nebuchadnezzar what will take place in the latter days. This was your dream and the visions in your mind while on your bed.'"*

Daniel gave the Lord credit first for what was about to happen. Eventually, after Daniel interpreted the dream correctly, the king paid homage to Daniel, rewarded him with gifts, and appointed him ruler over the province of Babylon. Daniel used his God-given skills in a powerful way and was promoted to a high-level leadership position.

Later on, Daniel was once again asked to interpret the king's dream. This time, however, the king provided all the details, so Daniel understood exactly what happened. In this particular situation, Daniel became concerned:

*"Then Daniel, whose name is Belteshazzar, was appalled for a while as his thoughts alarmed him. The king responded and said, 'Belteshazzar, do not let the dream or its interpretation alarm you.' Belteshazzar replied, 'My lord, **if only** the dream applied to those who hate you and its interpretation to your adversaries! The dream reveals such a terrible future that Daniel wishes it was for the king's enemy.'"*

—Dan. 4:19

If you've ever had to deliver bad news to your boss, you know Daniel's stress. He started his explanation by reminding the king that the God above is the one who provided Daniel with the understanding and ability to do what he does. After the details of the dream played themselves out in the king's life and things settled back to normal, the king turned to God and acknowledged his greatness by saying, *"Now I, Nebuchadnezzar, praise, exalt and honor the King of heaven, for all His works are true and His ways just, and He is able to humble those who walk in pride"* (Dan. 4:36).

Daniel took every opportunity to first give credit to God for his unique ability. However, Daniel also used the gift at work to do what the king had hired him to do. Regardless of the news being good, like the first interpretation, or bad, like the last interpretation, Daniel did his job well and shared his faith.

Although you may not be gifted with dream interpretation like Daniel, God has certainly equipped you with the necessary skills to do your job well. In addition, we all have a chance to appropriately speak about our faith at work as the opportunities present themselves.

If your work environment involves constantly dealing with people, consider displaying a Bible verse on your desk or phone that helps guide you in your interactions. I've heard people reference a Bible verse or two when someone asks them how they can maintain patience, joy, or encouragement. Simply sharing the verse and connecting it to what someone sees can make a big statement about your faith.

Earlier we covered the topic of purposeful prayer and how it can impact people around you. Over the course of my career, I've come across a number of stories about business people who were offered promotions only to ask for a bit of time to pray about the decision first. How would your boss respond if you asked for time to pray the next time he made you a big offer? An appropriate and humble request to pray and ask God for wisdom could be the one thing that prompts someone to ask you about your faith.

The most important thing to remember is that being ready to say something regarding your faith is a must if you're going to live your faith at work. Daniel could have simply done his job and honored God with how he did his work, but when he added the words that put the spotlight on God, the impact was more profound. The apostle Paul wrote in Romans 10:17, "*So faith comes from hearing, and hearing by the word of Christ.*" People can't hear anything if we don't say anything. God is ready to use our words to bring people to himself.

Gentleness and Respect

Speaking up is important, but speaking should be coupled with gentleness and respect. In 1 Peter 3:15, we read this great instruction for sharing our faith: *"But sanctify Christ as Lord in your hearts, always being ready to make a defense to everyone who asks you to give an account for the hope that is in you, yet with gentleness and reverence."* Those words, *gentleness* and *reverence* (i.e., *respect*), should be etched on our hearts. When you want to tell someone about your faith, use these words as guardrails to courageously have a conversation.

What I'm about to say may raise some eyebrows in the Christian community: I believe that street-corner preaching about hell and damnation doesn't work. Truthfully, I don't think it ever served the gospel message of Jesus well. I believe God can use anyone in any way to bring people to himself, but proclaiming the gospel in a way that is adversarial seems out of place. In reading 1 Peter 3:15 and examining the way the apostle Paul and others engaged in sharing the gospel, I can't find a good example where an in-your-face, heaven-or-hell message was effective.

I was leaving a sporting event one evening, walking back to the car with thousands of others, when we came across a group of street-corner evangelists. Their message had zero gentleness or reverence, and I couldn't help but wonder if they did more damage than good to the faith that evening. Again, only God knows the impact. For us, 1 Peter 3:15 offers powerful words to live by.

By definition, *gentleness* means being "kindly; amiable."[2] The Greek word used in 1 Peter 3:15 is *prautes* (prah-oo-tace), which means mildness, humility, and patience.[3] The point is that we should lead with gentleness when we share our faith.

The word *reverence* or *respect* used in 1 Peter 3:15 is the Greek word *phobos*, which means fear.[4] There is a reverence and an awe attached to this perspective of fear, and it typically includes a slight sense of inadequacy. When sharing our faith, it's easy to come across as self-righteous and all-knowing, and I believe the inclusion of this word is designed to help prevent that from happening.

Conversation Starters

We need to be prepared to say something with gentleness and respect, but what are some ways to have the critical conversations? What can we talk about that won't necessarily offend, but will likely open the door to the gospel message of Jesus? The examples below aren't exhaustive, and I am certain there are others, but these will get you started.

Share a Story

Sharing a story about a recent blessing in your life can be a great way to open the door for a faith conversation. Every year, my church sends a group of people to Haiti, taking the message of Jesus to people and helping them build homes, add on to schools, and conduct pastor training. As part of the trip, the team raises money to support the mission efforts. When they reach their goal, they have a powerful story to share about the blessings of God and how he provided for the trip. It's an easy story to share, and it can open the door for additional conversations about faith.

Share a Prayer

Share the power of prayer and how it has impacted your life. When we first moved to Houston, I had a number of people ask, "What brought you to Texas?" That simple question allowed me to explain my new job offer, my uncertainty about relocating my family, and the day I spent on the banks of the Chattahoochee River praying and searching my Bible for wisdom. By the end of that day, I had an unexplainable sense that we should move to Texas. Quiet prayer and time in my Bible was the difference maker, and sharing that story often opens the door to more faith conversations.

Share from Church

A simple comment about a recent church service or something that happened at church can be a great start to a conversation about faith.

As a resident of Friendswood, Texas, I often had to explain that our town was a suburb in South Houston. However, after Hurricane Harvey hit our area, more and more people knew exactly where Friendswood was located. The record-setting rain and devastating floods put our town and many others in the area front and center in the national news. The destruction was hard to comprehend. Yet, amid the destruction, our church (and many others across the city) mobilized people and resources for rescues and rebuilds. The work our church was doing opened up conversation after conversation about faith and the work God was doing.

Sharing your church stories doesn't have to be on the scale of a hurricane rebuild effort, but it's likely your church is participating in a variety of things designed to serve people. These activities are excellent conversation starters to understand the role faith plays in the lives of people around you.

Share the Bible

Another excellent conversation starter is the concept of biblical references showing up in the workplace. When I was a speaker at a college recruiting event, my topic was leadership versus management. I was sharing my experience with a group of high-potential college students. As I shared several long-held management truths, a student raised his hand to comment on a principle I'd mentioned. "I agree with what you said," he said, "because I once heard that there is nothing new under the sun." His point was that many leadership and management principles are timeless, at least the good ones. What got my attention was the comment about "nothing new under the sun." I asked the group if they knew where that saying came from, and no one was comfortable enough to answer. This gave me the opportunity to explain that Solomon wrote it in the book of Ecclesiastes. It was a simple opportunity to bring the Bible into the discussion. Later that day, I had a chance to circle back with the student who made the comment, and we had a great faith-filled conversation. Many of the best management and leadership principles have their foundation in the pages of the Bible. Referencing what God's word says to support something at work is a great transition into faith conversations.

Share Current Events

We can also use current events, new movies, and countless other areas of interest to find a connection to faith. Shortly after the movie *I Can Only Imagine* came out, I had the opportunity to talk about it with one of my students. The subject of recent movies came up in conversation, and that small opening provided a chance to share a bit of my personal story of coming to know Jesus.

The media covers story after story about tragedy, triumph, and controversial behaviors. These stories can serve as a backdrop for transitioning to a conversation about faith. Be willing to ask people what they think about current new stories. Listen for clues on where they might stand with faith. Look for opportunities to point out something that the Bible says on a topic to see if that prompts a deeper conversation. My experience has been that most people are very willing to share what they believe when we are willing to hear it with an open mind.

If we are willing and ready to engage in crucial conversations and remember to allow gentleness and respect to be our guide, God will create more opportunities to talk about faith than we ever thought possible.

9

Individual Invitations

My first real job that felt like a career opportunity required me to move from Dallas, Texas, to Cincinnati, Ohio. I had grown up in Texas and even went to college in Texas, so the idea of leaving was never on my radar. Despite my negotiation efforts to remain in Texas, my new boss made the final decision easy: move to Ohio or don't accept the job. I decided to move.

Driving into Cincinnati for the first time made me aware of a horrifying truth: I had no friends, no family, and no social contacts in the area. From a personal perspective, I was alone. Fortunately for me, I worked with a man named Larry, who invited me to a picnic at his home the first day I was in town. Larry had been in the industry for almost 40 years, so he knew a few things about transitions. On top of that, he had moved several times over the course of his career, making him aware of the anxiety associated with big change.

Despite what I knew about Larry, I was less than enthusiastic about the invite. I wouldn't know anyone, and, given Larry was more than double my age, I didn't expect to make any connections. But Larry knew what he was doing: he invited several people who worked with one of our clients, and they were closer to my age. I quickly made connections, and the fear and uncertainty about the move began to fade. That single event had a significant impact on my life, and it made those first few weeks in a new place seem less intimidating.

Years later, when my business partner and I opened our stores in Arizona, we created a similar experience for the team members we hired from out-of-state. Our goal was to make the transition to a new place as smooth and as comfortable as possible. We wanted them to feel part of a family in our company. The central event of the year was Thanksgiving dinner.

Each Thanksgiving, we invited many new hires to our house to celebrate. In most cases, the new hires had families in other parts of the country, and since Thanksgiving is a big sales time, it was difficult for people to get enough time off to head home. Our goal was to create a family atmosphere with our team in order to make the separation a little easier. We experienced significant growth because of this atmosphere and our funding, and we had a lot of fun. The annual holiday invite was one of the reasons why. Our company felt like a family, and those individual invitations meant a lot to everyone who participated.

Extending an invitation to others sends a powerful message: "I want to include you." Consider times when you were invited to something and how it made you feel. Probably pretty good. What about the times you did the inviting? That was probably even more rewarding. Invitations are good ideas, until the topic of church comes up. The idea of inviting someone to church can stir up all kinds of resistance and apprehension.

What keeps us from taking the step? In some cases, it might be proximity. In today's commuting world, many people don't work near where they attend church. As a result, many people feel the invite would be declined. In other cases, there are many workplaces that prohibit anything related to faith. Some have even lost their jobs for sharing their faith at work. Fortunately, these situations are few and far between. Regardless of the workplace environment, there are ways to bring your faith to work that don't violate policy and do demonstrate a level of respect and gentleness that Jesus himself would encourage.

I have a good friend named Steve who worked for one of those companies where faith was prohibited. He explained it to me this way: he wasn't directly forbidden to speak about faith, but he opened himself up to complaints if he was forward or bold with too much religion. Steve was a follower of Jesus, and he realized that compartmentalizing his faith wasn't an option. If he was going to be a Christian, then he needed to do it on Sunday at church, Monday through Friday at work, Saturdays, and every morning and evening at home.

Steve came across a creative way to bring faith into the conversation by using the individual invitation approach with a few people on his team. Every year, the Willow Creek Association puts on a Leadership Summit that features some of the top speakers in business, non-profit groups, and other fields. The goal is to impart leadership wisdom and equip everyone with tools to maximize their influence at work and at home. The heavy emphasis on building leadership skills gave Steve an idea. He decided to invite three of his coworkers to participate in the event. Since the agenda and focus were leadership and business, it was a perfect scenario for the group.

Out of the gate, Steve received great feedback from those who participated. Because they could apply what they learned at work, it was a win-win for everyone. Eventually, Steve was able to convince his organization to cover the cost for those who wanted to attend. Yes, it was a business event, but the structure placed the name of Jesus and the principles of the Christian faith front and center. The Bible itself says in Isaiah 55:11, "*So will My word be which goes forth from My mouth; It will not return to Me empty, without accomplishing what I desire, and without succeeding in the matter for which I sent it.*"

God's word was going out through the speakers and the music at the leadership summit, and it would not return empty.

Steve said that one of his guys was so captured by the event that he pulled Steve aside to ask him about attending church. Evidently, the message and methods were exactly what this person needed to prompt him to act. Shortly after Steve's friend returned home, he found a new church and took his family with him on a weekly basis. God had used Steve, the conference, and many of the speakers to capture this man's heart, and his life was changed. The simple invitation made all the difference in the world.

Another thing that has kept me from personally extending an invitation was fear. Sometimes it was fear of the unknown: will they be interested or not? Other times, it was fear of how someone might judge me. In some cases, I had this fear that the invitation would be inconvenient. Regardless of the fear, I often let it keep me from a bold invitation. That kept me limping along with my faith at work for a number of years until God used a Bible study to get my attention.

Shortly after moving to Houston, I met with different people weekly to talk about business and, God willing, faith. Sometimes faith came up, but other times it didn't. Either way, I was patient and hopeful that a few of my coworkers would come to know Jesus. Finally, after months of lunches, coffees, and other relationship-building times together, I had enough people interested in faith that we could start a Bible study. We blocked off time in the morning before the workday started, and our group began meeting in the office. It was the first time I had an opportunity like this, and I was grateful for the work God was doing both in me and in the people around me.

The study itself started off well; people were showing up weekly to read God's word and consider how we could apply what it teaches to our jobs. Every week we tackled a new topic, and everyone was participating. Then I showed up one morning to an empty meeting room. I knew I was a bit early, so I opened up my Bible and read while I waited for others to join. Then I waited. Twenty minutes after the proposed start time, I was still waiting. It was a no show, and I sat in that conference room wondering what in the world God was doing. Here I was ready and willing, but no one was interested. I asked God why, feeling a deep sense of disappointment and failure.

As I prayed, I was reminded of 1 Corinthians 3:6, where Paul says, "*God causes the growth*." Not Craig, but God. I have spent most of my career in sales, and I once heard someone translate that verse in salesperson terms. He said, "In sales, you get paid for the close; but with God, you get paid for the ask." The point was that our role is to show up and ask, but God determines the outcome. As I sat at that conference table in that empty room, I realized God was looking for me to show up and be ready. I was ready, and I was present. Right then I realized my fear was grounded in my hope of a positive outcome. I was caught up with the results; I wanted to produce. God reminded me that day that he will handle the results if I am willing to be available!

There are many ways to extend invitations to people in your circle of influence so that they are exposed to the teachings of Jesus. The key is to trust God and take steps to invite people. Jesus is looking for us to simply make the ask; he will handle the rest.

10

Embrace Endurance

There was a time in our society when waiting for things was part of the deal. We waited for letters to come in the mail, we waited in lines to purchase things, and we waited for people to get home. The idea of waiting was simply the way things were. But things have changed dramatically over the years. Technology has ushered in an era of quick responses and reduced wait times. Now, waiting is more an annoyance than anything else.

Today, we are accustomed to getting things immediately. The instant-gratification mindset has changed the expectations people have for response times. Like most people, I am grateful for the way technology has evolved and how it has improved the time it takes to do certain things. I was reminded of this when I recently completed the renewal for my truck registration. The notice came to me in the mail, and I immediately went online to complete the process. Compare that to the old school way of carving out a full day to make the pilgrimage to the local DMV, and you have reason to celebrate.

Another spectacular innovation has been the download. We can download music, software, books, event tickets, and countless other items. We can get really cool things right away. I love the fact that I can go online and buy what I want on the fly. We often buy tickets on the way to the movies—an efficient tool for a night out. Prior to the download phenomenon, most people waited in lines and often tested their patience with the rest of the crowd. Who in their right mind would want to go back to a day where we wait, wait, wait for the things we want? Not this guy.

Unfortunately, there is a dark side to this instant-gratification lifestyle. The biggest challenge is that we expect immediate returns, feedback, or results. It's easy to take this same mindset and apply it to every arena of our lives, including our faith at work.

Consider this situation:

You've been praying about a coworker and hoping for the opportunity to share Jesus with her. You have daily interactions with her, and you've even had lunch together. Over the course of your relationship, you've dropped a few hints about your faith, and you've even shared something you heard at church following a great sermon. Despite your covert faith sharing, you are still not clear where she stands, and you are eager to share the good news of Jesus.

Finally, the day comes. You're having lunch and the topic of faith comes up during the conversation. After you share a bit of your own story, she says that she's just not sure about this whole God thing. You share a few Bible verses and maybe even draw a diagram or two on a piece of paper, and you're convinced it's time for her to surrender to Jesus. As you unfold the simple message of salvation, she's open and engaged. You get to the big question: "Are you ready to surrender to Jesus today?" But she responds, "No."

It's likely you will feel rejected and disappointed. There is also a chance this interaction changes your relationship for a period of time. It might feel awkward, given the results. In fact, you might consider keeping your faith conversations to a minimum to let things settle a bit. You tried, but it just didn't work.

I had this happen to me, and I learned a valuable lesson in trusting God and waiting for him to move.

I had an opportunity to grab lunch with two guys from work who'd been on my prayer list for a period of time. We worked closely together, and they were always open to faith-based conversations. Although we never talked about specific topics, we always chatted generally about church or shared a few wise quotes. I really felt as though God was working in their lives, so I was especially excited about this particular lunch meeting. Our time together started with the typical business conversation, and I was concerned we weren't going to get to the faith stuff. I kept looking for an opportunity to bring Jesus into the discussion until finally there was a window. I shared what surrendering to Jesus had done in my life and followed with a simple presentation of the gospel message: we all have sin, sin separates us from God, and there is no way to bridge the separation on our own. Each of the guys stayed engaged until we got to the invitation. I asked if there was anything standing in the way of surrendering to Jesus now. To my surprise, they each declined. They casually shifted the conversation away from faith and back to business.

I had no idea how it happened, and I had no idea how to get back to the reason I thought we were together. It was so frustrating! I'd been praying and finally had a chance to share my faith, yet they said no. I thought I'd missed the opportunity, that it would take a miracle to get these guys into a faith conversation in the future. Thankfully, the God I serve is in the miracle business.

Several months after that lunch discussion, I was having coffee with one of the guys. We were talking about work and family things when out of the blue he said, "Do you remember when you asked if there was anything keeping me from surrendering my life to Jesus? Well, I've been thinking about it, and I would like to do that today." I was shocked. I had no idea what happened, and I wasn't sure why he wanted to make the decision now. But I walked him through a prayer to surrender his life to Jesus, and just like that, my friend was saved.

The frustration and disappointment I'd experienced before were replaced with joy and gratitude. It was also a powerful reminder that God's timing is perfect and that I have no idea what God is doing in someone's life to turn them to Jesus. In this case, it took a few months, and I've since had experiences that took longer. In some instances, I'm still praying for people who've not made a decision for Jesus. My hope is that God will open their hearts to himself and that they will know the joy that comes from following Jesus. Until then, I keep praying and keep looking for opportunities.

Endurance, or staying the course, is a key principle God challenges us to pursue. It's also a critical principle to apply when it comes to living your faith at work. In Hebrews 12:1, we read, *"Therefore, since we have so great a cloud of witnesses surrounding us, let us also lay aside every encumbrance and the sin which so easily entangles us, and let us run with endurance the race that is set before us."* Run with endurance the race that is set before us. He's referring to the race of life. In this case, the word *endurance* means "the fact or power of enduring or bearing pain, hardships,"[1] like a marathon runner steadily moving forward to the destination.

One of my favorite stories around a steady and prayerful approach to God's work is from the life of Dawson Trotman. Trotman was the founder of the Navigators, a ministry providing one-on-one discipleship to Christians.

In his biography *The Navigator*, Robert D. Foster shares a story about Dawson claiming a promise from God in Jeremiah 33:3: "'Call to Me and I will answer you, and I will tell you great and mighty things, which you do not know." According to the story, Dawson and his good friend Walt decided to meet every morning for two hours to pray about the work they believed God had called them to do. At first, their prayers focused on reaching people in every state in the US. Over time, they started asking God to enable them to reach people in every country. They were praying for 12 hours a week and an additional 3 hours on Sundays! Can you imagine a commitment to praying for 15 hours a week? Foster records what happened after 42 days of prayer:

> At the end of forty-two days, they felt the burden lift, and they began to thank God that he had heard them and was going to fulfill what He had promised. During the six weeks they had spent over one hundred hours in prayer in the hills together with God, asking Him to use them to win and train men for His glory around the world. Little did they realize what was in store for them in the years to come![2]

I'm not sure how you feel about committing more than one hundred hours to prayer over the next six weeks, but that is a powerful example of endurance! God's answers to their prayers unfolded over the course of several years, but the commitment to seek God took faith and an unwavering commitment to prayer. Is there a promise from God you've considered claiming? The example of Dawson and Walt is both inspiring and convicting for me.

The Bible teaches that patience is part of the Christian faith. Waiting for God is a major theme in Psalms. In light of that, it's important to remember that relationships take time to build. This is especially true in the workplace, as it is easy to let the work part of your interaction with people be the only point of connection. I've learned this the hard way over the years, and it's been something I'm still working to get past.

Early in my career, my sole interest for people centered on the business we did together. As a young salesperson, I considered it my job to find the business needs, look for solutions, and work to close new sales with every customer. For me, that meant asking a lot of questions about a customer's professional goals, their organization's challenges, and the competitive pressure they were under. I took a lot of pride in the depth of understanding I had with each of my customers. Often, I was able to turn that understanding into a business opportunity for our company. This same approach carried over to the people on our sales team. I asked questions to understand their territories, which customers were the most difficult, and what products sold well across our region. I knew a lot of business information about people, but I knew very little personal information about them. It's not that they were unwilling to share parts of their life with me; I just wasn't asking about them. And when their personal lives came up, I wasn't listening. I was driven toward information that would help the business. That drive prevented me from developing a complete relationship with people.

A complete relationship allows a person to share any part of their life and know that they have been heard. This openness builds trust and, over time, can create opportunities to talk about things beyond the work-based topics. There are certainly people who want to share too much, or who talk about everything except work-related topics, but those are the exceptions and not the norm. If you are not sure where you stand on this topic, consider these questions:

- Do you know the name of your coworker's spouse and children (or if they have children)?
- Do you know if your coworkers have siblings and where they grew up?
- Do you know where your coworkers live and what hobbies they enjoy?
- Have you ever invited any of your coworkers to see your home or to meet your family?

These questions are basic, but they highlight the point. It's easy to keep the relationships in the workplace about the work, but that is not God's way. Jesus offered a powerful example by how he quickly got to know people on a personal level. Take the example of Zacchaeus in Luke 19:1–10.

Zacchaeus was a tax collector. During Jesus's time, tax collectors were seen as the worst of the worst. They had a reputation (warranted in many cases) for misusing their tax collection privilege to extort money from innocent people. They were protected by the Roman government, so they had free reign to over-tax in the interest of padding their own bank accounts. Needless to say, the tax collector was not a popular person to have at the dinner table.

In Luke's story, Zacchaeus was interested in seeing what this Jesus person was all about, so he found Jesus, who was entering the city of Jericho. Because Zacchaeus was unusually short, he had to climb a tree to get a glimpse of Jesus. Immediately upon entering the area, Jesus saw him and said, "I must stay at your house today."

The people who witnessed the exchange were shocked. The religious people of the day couldn't believe that Jesus would go to the home of a sinner! What in the world was he doing? Well, if you understand the life and teaching of Jesus at all, then this shouldn't surprise you. He cared about people, and he knew that a relationship starts with being willing to meet a person where they are. In this case, Jesus literally wanted to meet Zacchaeus at his house. He wanted to spend time with a tax collector in the most personal and private place in his life: his house. Jesus wanted a relationship, and he was an expert at meeting people where the relationship could best be cultivated.

A commitment to endurance is crucial for building relationships today. Most of us don't have the draw power that Jesus had back in his day when people came to him in droves. However, we all have influence and access to people inside our circle. People we interact with every day represent relationship opportunities. By definition, a relationship is simply a connection to people. I think our society has over-complicated the notion of relationships by placing so much emphasis on the depth of relationships. We over-think what a relationship is, and many people shy away from them because of a fear of commitment.

The fact is that you have a relationship to some level with everyone who crosses your path on a fairly regular basis. The only decision you really make is which ones you will invest more of yourself into. This is why embracing endurance is so important for living our faith at work. Building relationships takes time and is often impacted by circumstances outside of our control. When we take a long-term view and focus more on investing in the relationships that God has placed around us, we allow our lives to be seen. When we are following Jesus and living the way he's asked us to live, it will be noticed.

I didn't grow up on a farm, but I have always appreciated the agricultural illustrations in the Bible. The example of a farmer and the work it takes to produce a crop is one of the more powerful illustrations. If you've ever tried to grow anything, then you can relate. It's slow, unpredictable, and tedious. But on the other hand, when you have successfully harvested, it is rewarding, affirming, and, in many cases, delicious! I can appreciate the apostle Paul's description in 1 Corinthians 3:6–7: "*I planted, Apollos watered, but God was causing the growth. So then neither the one who plants nor the one who waters is anything, but God who causes the growth.*" Paul says that God is the one who causes growth in people. His role, Apollos's role (friend of Paul's), and *our* role is to "*plant seeds and water.*"

To be clear, the seed and water are the gospel message that Jesus came to earth, died on a cross, and rose from the dead to pay for our sin so that we can have a relationship with God. We are doing the work of the farmer. To apply that to faith at work, we need to foster relationships, share the seeds of the gospel message, and water those seeds by how we live. Ultimately, God is responsible for the growth. Waiting is why endurance is so important. We never know when growth will come, so until it happens, we keep farming the fields with great attention and care.

When my friend and I had an opportunity to start our own business and open a chain of mattress stores in Arizona, we discussed people we needed to get the business started. We knew a few of my family members would be part of the team, but we really wanted someone with retail and industry experience. It didn't take long before we both came to the same conclusion: we needed to get Chris on our team. Chris worked for one of our customers and was very talented as a buyer and an overall business manager. He would be perfect for what we needed. After a series of discussions and persuasive conversations from my business partner, Chris agreed to join our team. Hiring him proved to be a great move for our newly formed business because his direct and candid style combined with his business knowledge helped shape our company. He was a great asset!

It was during the early stages of launching and establishing the business that I surrendered my life to Jesus. My decision wasn't based on any difficult circumstance, though we were in over our heads in operating our new venture. My decision came after I heard a message at church that explained the difference between "religion of God" and "relationship with God." It opened my eyes in a powerful way. I knew then that I wanted a relationship with the one who created me. At the end of the message, I confessed my sin, acknowledged my belief that Jesus rose from the dead, and surrendered leadership of my life to him. It would take me a bit of time to make sense of what had happened, but my life was changed that day, and it has never been the same since.

My newfound faith in Jesus drew me to the Bible and started me on a path to know God more deeply, living a life surrendered to him. I shared my experience with as many people as were willing to listen. It was amazing to watch the work God was doing during those early days of faith.

One day, I had the opportunity to talk with Chris about the message of Jesus. He had seen what was happening with people on our team, and he knew that faith in Christ had become an important part of our lives. One day, while Chris and I were at lunch, the conversation shifted to things of faith. I had hoped for an opportunity to present Jesus to him and invite him to consider surrendering his life. Unfortunately, things didn't go exactly as I had planned.

During our lunch, I covered the basics of sin and how it separates us from God, and I explained that Jesus is the only way to bridge the gap. Despite the presentation, Chris wasn't interested. He made it clear that although he respected my faith and the team's decision to follow Christ, it wasn't for him. He saw no need for a Savior, and I couldn't change his mind. I left our lunch that day disappointed and questioning my ability to properly share the message of Jesus with someone. Once again, I was reminded of what Paul taught in 1 Corinthians 3. God causes the growth; I'm simply called to plant seeds and water.

We continued to operate that business for another few years and Chris continued to be one of our top leaders. We had good times and bad, but Chris stayed loyal and committed. He also stayed away from anything that had to do with faith in Jesus. I continued to pray that God would open his heart to Jesus, but nothing changed.

It's been almost 17 years since that conversation with Chris. For several years, we didn't have any interaction because we went separate ways with work. However, as only God can do, our paths crossed again when I went to work for Mattress Firm in Houston. We ended up working together on a fairly regular basis and periodically talked about life and even faith here and there. As of the writing of this book, I am not sure if Chris ever chose to follow Jesus, but I know he and his wife attend church, and there may be a day when he decides to make that choice. I'm sure our paths will cross again, and I will keep praying that God will open his heart to believe and receive the message of Jesus. I want to embrace endurance knowing that God's timing is always perfect. He can turn a heart toward himself at any time.

Embracing endurance in your life might look just like my experience. Keep praying and looking for opportunities with that one person who seems resistant to God's message. Who knows when God will act! Endurance might also be praying for a small group of people you interact with every day who have shown no interest in Christianity. Or, endurance might be the continued resistance to bending the truth or compromising on something that everyone around you says is OK.

Whatever your challenge, there are a number of ways you can embrace endurance and strive to actively live your faith at work. One of those ways is to surround yourself with people in the workplace who share your same passion for faith.

Finding a like-minded person or a small group of people who are serious about their faith can be an incredible resource. They can encourage you and hold you accountable for living the principles of Christianity on a daily basis. God designed us to need each other, and the workplace offers the same powerful community opportunity that a small group from your church can offer. In fact, my friend Kent once described his team of coworkers as his "workplace small group." That's a powerful picture of like-minded believers.

Kent works at a major hospital owned by the state of Texas. He is a high-ranking and highly influential member of their team. Since it's a state institution, you can imagine the limitations on faith-based conversations and activities. Despite the tight boundaries for open faith, Kent has found a way to live his faith at work, and it came through a unique relationship with his team.

Kent has a coworker who has a heart for serving Jesus every hour of every day. She speaks openly about her faith when the opportunity presents itself, and she has consistently encouraged Kent in his own journey with the Lord. She and two other members of the team keep each other accountable for how they speak to others and how they conduct themselves in meetings. They regularly talk about Bible verses and what God is doing in each of their lives. When they get the chance, they pray with others at work and try to reflect the qualities of Jesus to both coworkers and patients. This small band of Christ followers is fighting the good fight at work. They're like an elite group of Navy Seals dropped behind enemy lines, bringing the good news of Jesus to people in need. Don't get me wrong: I'm not suggesting their hospital is filled with enemies. But the enemy himself is interested in keeping the message and hope that Jesus offers out of that place. This small group of soldiers is serving on the front line to keep Jesus and what he stands for front and center in the lives of everyone they encounter. The encouragement and accountability they offer each other is powerful.

Another way to find help with endurance is through a prayer partner. This is someone in your workplace who can commit to praying with you for the office and the people in the office. I have covered the power of prayer in several places throughout this book, and having a prayer partner is a way to make purposeful prayer even more of a focus.

During my time as an executive at Mattress Firm, I found a prayer partner in a wonderful lady named Joi (pronounced Joy). Joi came to our company from another industry, so she had her challenges gaining credibility among the people on her team. As I watched her work and heard others describe her approach, I could see she was genuinely interested in people as individuals and not simply as workers. She asked about their family, hobbies, and motivation. She spent time working next to her team and ultimately earned their respect and admiration.

Joi is also a sold-out follower of Jesus. Shortly after Joi and I had our first faith conversation, I knew she was living her faith at work. She was based in North Carolina, and I was in the Houston office, so our paths didn't cross often. When they did, we often talked about what God was doing in the lives of people at the company. Over time, we collaborated on prayers for certain people. Every May, prior to the big summer selling season, we asked God to protect our teams and guide us as we stewarded the company he had entrusted to us. Our shared prayer was always a powerful reminder that neither of us was alone in the pursuit of showing Jesus at work.

Over time, more and more people came to know Jesus in our organization, and we looked forward to the annual leadership conference where we had a chance to gather as a group. Early on, three or four of us began gathering each morning during our conference to pray for the day. Each year, more and more people showed up. The last year of the conference, we started our mornings with anywhere from 20 to 30 people gathered to pray for the company, the leaders, and that God would be magnified. I never could have imagined so many people coming together at a company conference for the sole purpose of praying to Jesus. By embracing endurance, partnering in prayer, and asking God to open doors of opportunity, we were able to participate in the amazing work of Christ. It was an honor and a blessing.

Work demands we deliver results, but Jesus is far less demanding. He says that he will handle the results. He only calls us to obey. If we will live every part of our lives the way he has designed, we will have access to every promise he offers us in the Bible. Fight the good fight, run the race with endurance, and remember that Jesus has a reward waiting for you.

11

The Opportunity

In the movie *The Matrix*, the main character, Neo, meets Morpheus, the leader of a band of rebels. Morpheus has a prophetic vibe, and he presents Neo with a revolutionary perspective. He tells Neo that everyone is blinded from the truth and that he is a slave, born into bondage, born into a prison for his mind. He goes on to explain this idea of the matrix and wraps it up with an offer. He offers Neo a blue pill, with which, he says, "The story ends. You wake in your bed and you believe whatever you want to believe."[1] However, he can opt for the red pill, which means he stays in wonderland and will be shown "how deep the rabbit hole goes." Morpheus ends with this final statement: "Remember, all I am offering is the truth, nothing more."[2] Neo chooses the red pill and begins a series of awakenings culminating in his body being ejected from the pod where he'd been living and being retrieved by Morpheus and his crew. The entire movie is an apocalyptic battle between machines and the remaining human population with an intense connection between knowing the truth and freedom—both themes that are powerfully present in the Bible.

Choice is a powerful concept that God offers his creation. When we hear the message of Jesus, we have a choice whether to believe it and receive it. However, for those who have made that choice, living their faith at work becomes a responsibility. When we say yes to Jesus, we are saying yes to all he wants for our lives. You may be living your faith on Sundays and occasional weekdays but neglecting the charge to bring it to work. I understand that mindset. It's clean, easy, and allows you to live comfortably. But that is not God's intention. Followers of Jesus are challenged to live faith boldly, in a way that seeks God's full plan for our lives. It's the plan in which we put Jesus at the front of who we are and what we do, and allow our faith to direct our steps. God wants us to be refreshed, encouraged, and equipped on Sundays so that we are ready to continue the work he has given us to do. The Christian faith anchors our souls in Christ, and it's through an active faith that God continues to shape us into the person he designed us to be. Living your faith at work brings freedom from compartmentalizing your life. A willingness to share your faith with others keeps your eyes off of yourself.

A life that embraces the truth of what Jesus teaches offers so much more than what the world has to offer. In John 10:10, Jesus said, "*The thief comes only to steal and kill and destroy;* ***I came that they may have life, and have it abundantly***" (emphasis added). I find this verse to be one of the most encouraging and motivating verses ever written. The contrast between Jesus's purpose and the enemy's purpose is clear. Jesus came so that we can have an abundant life. The Greek word for "abundant" is *perissos*, which means "superior in quality and beyond measure." Beyond measure makes me think about the love I have for my wife and sons. If I tried to quantify it, I couldn't do it. The love I have for my family is beyond measure.

The abundant life in Jesus gets off track when we look at our lives and measure them with the standards of the world. The world says, "The more you have, the more you are blessed." Fortunately for us, Jesus doesn't measure "more" in terms of stuff or what we contribute. The abundance he provides is at the heart level, and as we surrender more of our lives to him, we shift from a self-centered way of living to a self-giving way of life. This shift can have a major impact on our lives as we seek to live our faith more boldly. This is especially true in the workplace. Living our faith at work opens the door to this same abundant life Jesus has available to us. It also changes the purpose for our work. Jesus offers tremendous benefits when we live our faith at work.

Living your faith at work gives a higher purpose to what you do. Jesus talked about his work in terms of purpose. In Luke 19:10, he said, *"For the Son of Man has come to seek and to save that which was lost."* In John 17:4, at the end of his life, Jesus referenced his work in prayer: *"I glorified you on the earth, having accomplished the work which You have given Me to do."* He came to save people, and he did the work which God had given him to do.

In Colossians 1:28–29, Paul writes about purpose: *"We proclaim Him, admonishing every man and teaching every man with all wisdom, so that we may present every man complete in Christ. For this purpose also I labor, striving according to His power, which mightily works within me."* Paul says he is living to tell others about Jesus, and to teach others the ways of Jesus so that they can become fully devoted followers. When we see the purpose of our work as both Jesus and Paul viewed it, then it becomes more than just a job. It becomes our platform for living out the Great Commission: the command for all of us to make disciples and teach people how to live in Christ. Our purpose becomes sharing the truth of Jesus with others. What could be more life-changing than that?

A number of years ago, I was introduced to the idea of "marketplace ministry," the notion that every follower of Jesus is a pastor in their workplace every day to the people around them. At first, I had a hard time with this idea because I grew up in a traditional church in which ministry was the pastor's job. He was responsible for teaching religion, and my job was to do what I could to live a life of good behavior. However, as I studied the Bible and watched others model a life of serving Jesus, I realized that it is my responsibility to be a "minister of the message of Jesus." I realized that there are a lot of people in my circle of influence who may never step into the four walls of a church building. How in the world will they have access to the message of the Bible? God used people like Paul, the tentmaker, to share the message of Jesus and build up the early church. He used people like Peter, the fisherman, to turn more people to the way of Christ. God continues to use people from ordinary backgrounds to spread the message of Jesus in extraordinary ways. He's been working in people's lives for more than two thousand years, and he will continue for years to come.

Living your faith at work brings a new purpose to what you do Monday through Friday, and it's a purpose worth pursuing. However, God doesn't stop there. He goes beyond providing purpose with our work. When we see our workplace as an arena to share the eternal message of salvation, we also change the impact of our work. Changing a person's destiny by sharing a powerful truth—that's work with purpose and impact!

I worked alongside a guy named Matt for a number of years. We worked on the sales team as counterparts, collaborated on projects after I moved to another department in the company, and got to be pretty good friends outside of work. For a long time, our relationship was mostly about work. Matt's kids were much younger than ours, and they lived on the other side of town from us, so our interactions were few and far between. Regardless, we had a lot of time together at work. Over the course of our relationship, Matt had surrendered his life to Jesus, and his decision brought a new dimension to our conversations. God worked in both of us over the course of several years, and I was blessed to call Matt a friend and brother-in-Christ.

Recently, Matt and I exchanged texts on Father's Day, wishing each other a good one and planning a time to grab lunch together. Then Matt wrote something to me that freshly reminded me of the impact God wants to make in our lives through people: "You have no idea how influential you are as a model for me as a father." He was right; I had no idea. Matt and I have known each other for a long, long time, and we have shared a good bit of life together. Most of it was during work hours, but we've talked about almost every topic that might come up in a conversation. I'm not sure what Matt has learned from my parenting. It could be some of the positive ways we've tried to raise our own kids, or it could be lessons from the mistakes along the way. But it really doesn't matter that I know. God knows. God used my life, the good and the bad, to impact another person. When I consider my relationship with Matt and the way God used it to encourage and shape both of us, it reminds me of the impact we can have on each other. When we live our faith at work and make ourselves available to people, God can use us in amazing ways.

If purpose and impact aren't enough to convince you to pursue living your faith at work, then I will give you one more reason: the rewards Jesus has waiting for us when we invest in his eternal work. I know this truth can be misunderstood and complicated. There have been entire books and massive commentaries written on the topic of rewards. I'm not going to unpack the concept, define the implications, or go into depth on the theology of rewards. This chapter is about the opportunities in front of us if we are willing to live our faith at work boldly, participating in the process of more people coming to know Jesus. Eternal rewards are part of that opportunity.

Before I go any further on rewards, I want to be clear on an important statement of theology. Please read this carefully: eternal salvation is a result of believing and receiving the grace Jesus offered through the death and resurrection of Jesus Christ. We cannot work our way to heaven. Rewards are based on works after we become followers of Jesus. Grace saves; works are rewarded.

The apostle Paul addresses the topic of rewards in 1 Corinthians 3. There are many passages in the Bible about rewards, but one of my favorites is here in 1 Corinthians. Paul wrote,

> *Now if any man builds on the foundation with gold, silver, precious stones, wood, hay, straw, each man's work will become evident; for the day will show it because it is to be revealed with fire, and the fire itself will test the quality of each man's work.* **If any man's work which he has built on it remains, he will receive a reward.** *If any man's work is burned up, he will suffer loss; but he himself will be saved, yet so as through fire.*
>
> —1 Cor. 3:12–15, emphasis added

One day, God will evaluate our works for quality. If the quality is good, he will reward us. If the quality is bad, no reward. It's important to understand that God is a rewarder of those who seek him (Heb. 11:6). When we actively participate in God's plan for us, we are seeking after him. If we participate in other's lives, we *must* seek God. Dealing with people can be challenging, exhausting, and frustrating. Depending on God and his strength is the very best way to live.

As you read through the Bible and consider what matters most to God, you will find two things: his Word, and his people. His words and people's souls will live into eternity. In light of that truth, if you are going to invest your life in anything, invest it in God's word and God's people. Nothing else is living past this life.

The workplace offers a compelling arena to invest in what God values most. When you see your work in light of God's word, you realize that he designed it from the beginning of time. He made us all to work, so that we could cultivate the world. In some cases, this might literally mean taking care of the land. In other cases, it might be your current job; and in other cases, it could be the work you do in your home to care for your family. The work you do can provide significant meaning and have powerful purpose when it is grounded in living out what was mentioned in a previous chapter. Remember, Jesus taught in Matthew 28:19–20: "*Go therefore and make disciples of all nations, baptizing them in the name of the Father and the Son and the Holy Spirit, teaching them to observe all that I commanded you; and lo, I am with you always, even to the ends of the age.*" Each of us has influence and relationships where we work. When we do our work the way God intended and view our workplace as a place to both show and share Jesus, we are working the way God intended.

Unlike the choice Neo was offered in *The Matrix*, those who have surrendered their lives to Jesus have an obligation to live their faith at work. Unfortunately, the culture today pressures Christians to leave their faith at home. We must each choose to take an active role in what God is doing in the places where we spend our time. We must decide to be part of what God is doing. In addition to participating in what God is doing in others' lives, we get to be changed in the process. Jesus lives in us for a purpose: to change us from who we are to who he planned us to be. In his book *Mere Christianity*, C.S. Lewis says it like this: "God did not intend to make us a better version of ourselves, but to produce a new kind of man."[3] Transformation is the by-product of full surrender to Jesus. Full surrender means living our faith fully in every arena of life. This includes the workplace. There has never been a better time in history to actively bring our faith to work. People are frustrated, confused, and overwhelmed by the pace of life. The truth of Jesus and the life he offers is like a tall, cold glass of delicious water on a hot day. It's refreshing, restorative, and gives us new life. Don't miss out on the opportunity to be part of what God wants to do in you and through you with the people you work with daily!

Acknowledgments

There are so many people who contributed to this book that it will be difficult to mention them all. This story unfolded over the course of the past 17 years as I was influenced and educated by countless others who modeled work with a God-filled purpose. I am so grateful for each of them!

There are a number of people who had a direct impact on finishing up this project. For starters, I want to thank my wife, April. She constantly encourages me and challenges me to keep pressing forward. She even read through an early version of the manuscript and provided great insight. She's an amazing gift from God, and I love living life with her.

I want to thank Casey Cease and the team from Lucid Books. Not only was their work excellent, but they are some of the nicest people I have worked with. They truly felt like a partner in the process of pulling this all together. It never ceases to amaze me what a great publishing partner can do with an average manuscript. Thank you, Megan, Laurie, Laura, and Sammantha. You all were fantastic!

I also want to thank my good friends Trevor, Daniel, Craig, and Rick for taking the time to read the early versions and provide valuable insights. You are each living your faith at work, making your help a huge blessing.

I would like to thank Gary Vander Wiele for his theology support. I am grateful for the time he committed to read through the transcript and provide expert perspective.

I owe special thanks to Winston who has modeled a life fully surrendered to Jesus since the day I first met him. He pointed me toward the Bible on a regular basis and challenged me to think. I'm so thankful for the way you invested in me over the years.

There are also countless friends and coworkers from Mattress Firm, The Harbor, and the University of Houston who have demonstrated living the Christian faith at work. You inspire me and push me to seek more of what Jesus has for me personally in the way you live. Thank you for being willing to let Jesus be seen in all you do.

Notes

Chapter 2: The State of Work

1. Dictionary.com, s.v. "work," accessed August 27, 2018, https://www.dictionary.com/browse/work.
2. Anna Robaton, "Why So Many American's Hate Their Jobs," CBS News, March 31, 2017, https://www.cbsnews.com/news/why-so-many-americans-hate-their-jobs/.
3. Ibid.
4. Ibid.

Chapter 3: Work as Worship

1. Amy Morin, "7 Signs You May Be a Workaholic," *Psychology Today*, April 28, 2015, https://www.psychologytoday.com/us/blog/what-mentally-strong-people-dont-do/201504/7-signs-you-may-be-workaholic.

Chapter 4: Showing Faith before Sharing Faith

1. See *Merriam-Webster.com*, https://www.merriam-webster.com; *Strong's Concordance*.
2. Dictionary.com, s.v. "integrity," accessed August 22, 2018, https://www.dictionary.com/browse/integrity.

Chapter 6: Lead with Love

1. Sigal Barsade and Olivia A. O'Neill, "Employees Who Feel Love Perform Better," Harvard Business Review, January 13, 2014, https://hbr.org/2014/01/employees-who-feel-love-perform-better.
2. Ibid.
3. Ibid.

Chapter 8: Courageous Conversations

1. Josh Duboff, "If You See Something, Say Something: The Homeland Security Equivalent of 'Just do it,'" May 10, 2010, New York Magazine, 65.
2. Dictionary.com, s.v. "gentleness," accessed August 27, 2018, https://www.dictionary.com/browse/gentleness.
3. *Strong's Concordance*, iPhone ed., v. 3.0.3.
4. *Strong's Concordance*, iPhone ed., v. 3.0.3.

Chapter 10: Embrace Endurance

1. Dictionary.com, s.v. "endurance," accessed August 27, 2018, https://www.dictionary.com/browse/endurance.
2. Robert D. Foster, *The Navigator* (Colorado Springs: Nav Press, 1983), 87.

Chapter 11: The Opportunity

1. Larry and Andy Wachowski, *The Matrix*, https://www.imsdb.com/scripts/Matrix,-The.html.
2. Wachowski, *The Matrix*, https://www.imsdb.com/scripts/Matrix,-The.html.
3. C.S. Lewis, *Mere Christianity* (New York: Harper Collins, 1980), 108.

About Soul Purpose Inc.

The Soul Purpose Inc. organization is dedicated to helping Christians discover how to live their faith at work and be active in what God has prepared for them (Eph. 2:10).

- **Keynote speaking**
  Craig brings enthusiasm, energy, and several decades of experience to thousands each year on the topic of faith at work. His practical communication style and engaging approach leave audiences challenged in the way they think and equipped to make the changes they desire.

- **Teaching**
  The Soul Purpose Inc. strategy can be customized into small group studies or large group presentations. Our team is ready to lead or provide the necessary material to gifted leaders so they can take the message of living your faith at work to their organizations.

- **Writing**
  Soul Purpose Inc. will create content for faith at work programs, including short articles, lengthy stories, and unique study resources.

Visit our website at soulpurposeinc.com to learn more about each of these opportunities to work with us!

Other books by Craig McAndrews:

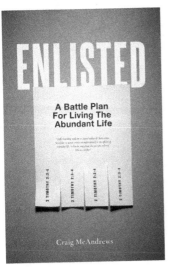

Do you want more out of life? *Enlisted* is about the abundant life God offers His people when they fully engage in serving Him. It was written to remind each of us that God has called us to a mission—one of purpose and opportunity. There are battles we will have to fight, but in the end, we are offered a life filled with meaning and impact! You will read about God's plans, Craig's own personal challenges with faith, and ultimately, a formula for engaging in active service. May you be inspired to take an active role in what God is calling YOU to do!

For more work by Craig McAndrews, visit craigmcandrews.com.

CPSIA information can be obtained
at www.ICGtesting.com
Printed in the USA
BVHW04s0501260918
528474BV00016B/91/P